I0755898

Nation of Lawyers

Nation of Lawyers

This is a work of both nonfiction and opinion. The author has taken great pains to be as accurate as possible with the factual information included in this book.

ISBN: 9781950381821

Printed in the United States

Published by Piscataqua Press
32 Daniel St., Portsmouth NH 03801
www.ppressbooks.com

Nation of Lawyers

How Lawyers, Aided by the U.S. Supreme Court, Manipulated U.S. Litigation to Enrich Only Themselves over the Past 50 Years.

Carl Arthur Henlein

INTRODUCTION

OPENING STATEMENT

From the beginning of America, lawyers have enjoyed a long and respected history. Our legal system became the most admired in the world. Lawyers were ethical, professional and respected by the public. Then they began filing lawsuits to enrich themselves. They decided to challenge the four bedrock, long-standing principles of our esteemed legal system. First, they wanted to file multiple, unnecessary lawsuits without being responsible to pay anything if they lost; second, they wanted to grab a lot of their clients' money as fees when it was paid to their clients in their lawsuits; third, they wanted to advertise their services and look like car salesmen while doing it; fourth, they wanted to expand class action suits so they could file bigger and more costly lawsuits, allowing them to claim excessive fees. These five aberrations undermined our admired, existing legal system.

None of this was permitted until, case by case, the lawyers began able to feather their own nests. Next, they wanted to influence the politicians to pick the judges that suited their purposes. So, they penetrated the places where laws are made. They control 60% of the U.S. Senate, where Federal Court judges are confirmed. Finally, they wanted the insurance industry to pay for it all. In sum, the lawyers wanted more money — a lot more money — for themselves. Their long-standing ethical responsibility to represent their clients was influenced by greed.

Surprisingly, the U.S. Supreme Court supported them in every case. A majority of the Justices gave them everything they asked for. So, the Supreme Court opened wide the doors for these new money-making aberrations to thrive. As a result, lawyers have been enriching themselves in these ways for 50 years and they continue to do so, without limits. Because lawyers govern themselves, and the Supreme Court agreed to allow them to do so, there is nothing to stop them. They push aside any effort from any direction to restrain them. Today, like the proverbial foxes, they oversee the hen house. The once admired U.S. civil justice system has become corrupted, expensive and unfair. No one admires it and no country copies it.

As a result of these aberrations, the scales of justice have tilted badly in the U.S. Over five decades, the number of lawyers multiplied nearly 5-fold to 1,400,000, more than all the other countries in the world combined. Collectively, they are extracting a massive sum of money from the economy. You don't always see it, but you are paying thousands of your dollars to them indirectly each year; when you pay for medical care, buy a product or buy insurance, for instance.

I am a retired trial lawyer. I have an insider's view as to how this happened and what it means for America's future. During my decades of trial practice in 17 of the biggest lawsuits in history, I was too deeply involved to perceive it, although it was going on all around me. But with time to reflect and hindsight, I see it now. It is like the fable about the blind man who meets an elephant. He touches a leg (is it a tree?), a trunk (is it a snake?), a tusk (is it made of ivory?), but he cannot see the entire elephant. Only hindsight allowed me to see what the lawyers accomplished. You will have the advantage of foresight, seeing how these aberrations occur and harm our legal system throughout my cases. I believe you will conclude, as I have, that the United States has become a nation of lawyers.

IN THE BEGINNING: 1776

America was founded with "blood, sweat and tears" by defeating England in the Revolutionary War. At that time, England was ruled by a King who governed for life. The war ended that tyrannical monarchy in the U.S. We paid a dear price to overthrow the British King. Historians estimate more than 27,000 patriots were killed, wounded or died from diseases in the eight-year war. This number may seem small today, but in 1776, less than 25,000 people lived in New York City (10 million live there now) and there were only 13 struggling Colonies rather than 50 robust states.

When the Founding Fathers gathered in Philadelphia, post war, to establish a new democratic government, they had suffered too much under the yoke of King James. So, their focus was to create "a nation of laws, not of men." The Founders established a basic principle in the U.S. Constitution that the laws governing the people would be enacted by citizens. The elected members of government would serve 2-, 4- and 6-year terms, not for life. Thus, the laws would be continuously subject to the review and votes of the citizens. The Founders were brilliant men. This new democracy they created would become the most powerful and admired country in the world.

They decided that a "country of laws" required a legal system of courts, with judges selected by the voting citizens, not the King as in England. The U.S. Federal Court judges would be nominated by the elected President and confirmed by the elected Senate. The judges would interpret the laws passed by the citizens and oversee legal disputes, *i.e.,* lawsuits between citizens, with each party represented by a lawyer. The Founders made the U.S. Supreme Court the ultimate authority on the law. The Constitution created the highest Court, but the elected Congress determined its authority so it could not seize power, like a King. There would be checks and balances in this democracy. The U.S. would be a "nation of laws" overseen by courts of esteemed judges.

The new civil justice system would need lawyers to present cases before citizen juries and argue the laws before judges in court. The primary drafter of the Constitution was a lawyer, Thomas Jefferson. The Founding Fathers intended to enable lawyers to be the unfettered representatives of the people; to that purpose, more than half of them were lawyers. In sum, they put their trust in lawyers — among the Founding Fathers, the 32 lawyers were men of great integrity. Lawyers would be at the forefront of protecting "a nation of laws."

In an early and famous opinion written by U.S. Supreme Court Chief Justice John Marshall, he stated, "*The government of the United States has been emphatically termed a government of laws and not of men.*" (Emphasis added.) *Marbury v. Madison*, 103 U.S. 537 (1896). Decades later, Abraham Lincoln (a respected lawyer) is attributed with saying, "*the government is of the people, by the people and for the people.*"

As "a nation of laws," the U.S. grew and prospered for over 240 years. The judges were esteemed; the lawyers practiced with integrity and were respected by the public. The United States civil justice system grew to exceed the visionary ideals of the Founders. *It was beyond good!*

Over time, the legal history of the U.S. started to change, but not for the better. The lawyers attacked long-standing legal principles that restrained their conduct and, therefore, restricted their ability for unlimited financial gain. The Supreme Court cast aside history, common sense and integrity to support them. As a result, today's civil justice system has fallen prey to self-centered abuses by lawyers and the errors of the Supreme Court. How this happened is complicated. It has many parts and did not take place overnight. It is not a short or simple story.

Today, lawsuits are growing in extraordinary numbers.

Every day there are new filings, everywhere. This massive litigation burden is out of control and costly. For just one example, as you will read later, *it is estimated unnecessary litigation expenses cost your healthcare system over one trillion dollars annually*. Think about that sum, one trillion dollars. What advances could be made in medicine with the money the lawyers are squandering, year after year? In addition, the aroma of big money is attracting new lawyers, so they are multiplying like rabbits; *about 40,000 new lawyers arrive each year* (that is more lawyers than France has in total). These two examples are but the tip of the iceberg of my exposé.

I note with interest that many of you are aware and concerned with this growing problem; the public's approval rating of lawyers is only 18% and falling. Sadly, the U.S. has become a nation of lawyers, not laws.

MY JOURNEY AS A TRIAL LAWYER: 1964

This is my story. It will draw back the curtain for you to see the complexities of U.S. litigation. It reveals the expanding problems existing today, with a likely bad ending. You can judge for yourself if, in fact, U.S. litigation has become a tar pit.

My law practice began in 1964 with one of the best law firms in Louisville, Kentucky. It had 16 lawyers and my salary was $4,800. My wife earned more money teaching the 5th grade in school. Imagine a society that valued teachers more than young lawyers. The Louisville-based law firm I retired from had 534 lawyers and salaries starting at $110,000. (I discuss this later in the chapter Lawyers, Lawyers and More Lawyers.) After a few years of general practice, I discovered I had some talent as a trial lawyer. So, my career took a turn into general litigation. I was defending product liability lawsuits for the firm's major clients like U.S. Steel, G.E., Firestone, Chevron, LG&E, Brown & Williamson, and others. This took me into courtrooms to defend large corporations in jury trials.

Then two events changed everything. A tragic fire and a large explosion occurred producing enormous lawsuits. They were the Beverly Hills Supper Club fire tragedy in northern Kentucky in 1977, and the sewer explosion in Louisville, Kentucky in 1981. My Kentucky law firm was retained to defend both lawsuits. The Supper Club fire litigation defense — which lasted 5 years — became my springboard. After it, I defended large U.S. corporations in massive lawsuits in New York City, Des Moines, Iowa, and Las Vegas, Nevada. That was just the beginning; many more massive lawsuits would follow. My new practice carried me far away from Louisville, into courtrooms across the U.S. and beyond, for more than three decades. As you travel with me, you will learn the recent history of U.S. litigation and see what has corrupted it.

You may be aware of some of my famous cases. They included lawsuits over terrorist attacks, *i.e.,* the Oklahoma City Bombing and the World Trade Center collapse, fires in large hotels like the MGM Grand Hotel and nightclubs like the Beverly Hills Supper Club that killed 600+ and injured 2,000+ innocent guests, as well as a fire on board an Air Canada plane that killed dozens of passengers. They included lawsuits filed against essential products like silicone breast implants, paint, tires, refrigerators, asbestos, and more. They were labelled "Mass Torts." A Mass Tort is a lawsuit(s) with huge claims with many claimants. They are some of the biggest lawsuits in the civil justice system. They are always large, complex, difficult and interesting. I will share some of my experiences of these Mass Tort lawsuits and trials with you.

LOUISVILLE SEWER EXPLOSION: 1981

I will begin with the Louisville sewer explosion litigation which was the second case in my Mass Tort career.

On February 13, 1981, a sewer line explosion in Louisville, Kentucky destroyed four miles of the city's sewers and disrupted nine miles of the city's streets. Two miles of the underground gas distribution pipes and water lines were destroyed, leaving parts of Louisville without these services. A large number of buildings were damaged, many businesses were interrupted, and 48 chimneys collapsed. Only four people were injured by the explosion that occurred when a car drove over a manhole; the heat of the car exhaust ignited the leaking explosive gas from the sewer. It was at 5:16 a.m. when the streets were deserted. Thus, a major personal injury disaster was avoided.

The three immediate suspects of the cause were the Metropolitan Sewer District (for the possible accumulation of the sewer gas), Standard Oil Company, now Chevron (for a possible gasoline tank farm leak four blocks away) and Louisville Gas and Electric Company (for a possible natural gas pipeline leak.) My partner, John McCall, and I represented all three companies in a common defense. Our immediate investigation revealed we could be confident none of these companies were the cause. Nevertheless, more than 17,000 claimants filed a class action lawsuit against these three companies in the United States District Court for the Western District of Kentucky in Louisville, Kentucky.

Three days later, John McCall and I proceeded to the largest explosion crater in the street to enter the sewer with our experts. We each took with us a professional sampler to obtain residue to analyze, a video cameraman to record what we saw and an explosion expert to attempt to determine the cause of the explosion. These two teams would be our forensic teams for the lawsuit defense. The local TV stations and media learned of our visit to the explosion site and appeared to report on it.

We arrived at the scene around 2:00 p.m. and all the local television stations were already recording our activity. Because I was aware that the TV cameras would be present, I wore my dark blue suit, a white shirt and red tie instead of work clothes. I only wore that suit for special occasions, *i.e.* trial opening statements and closing arguments, funerals and weddings. We all donned high rubber boots/waders before being hooked to a harness to be lowered into the gaping sewer crater by an overhead crane. We were lowered into the sewer, which was flowing downstream. It had about two feet of flowing sewer water, rich with what sewers are built to transport.... Disgusting! I assembled my team and preceded upstream to collect samples while videoing the damage. John and his team went downstream. About 15 yards upstream, while looking at the ceiling where explosion residue appeared to be present, I stumbled, slipped and fell headfirst into the stream. It was now time for me to leave the sewer.

A great stir began above the crater because the lead defense lawyer, me, was now coming out. Anticipation was high that I had an announcement to make about the cause of the sewer explosion. All the television cameras were focused on the ground level opening of the crater as I, hooked up to the crane harness, began to rise out of the hole. And rise I did. I am 5 feet 11 inches in height, but with my waders filled with sewer effluent — I now appeared to be over 7 feet tall. On and on I continued to emerge from the hole. The crane finally deposited me on the ground with a loud slushing sound as sewer water poured out of my waders. I was lying in a large pond of sewer refuse that I had made for myself. It was all captured live for the Louisville evening news programming. This was not the best of days for me or my lucky suit. I gathered and excused myself to leave the scene.

My fellow trial lawyers, for quite a long period of time,

reminded me that they had seen TV evidence that I was indeed full of shit. The sewer explosion was a wonderful opportunity for me to be named a lead lawyer for three of the largest corporations in Kentucky in a large Mass Tort. But as you will hear me say often, "beware the law of unintended consequences." My blue suit recovered and served me well.

Long story short, we soon had in our sights a culprit for the spill that blew up the sewers. We developed a claim against the Ralston Purina plant, seven miles upstream, for releasing thousands of gallons of hexane overflowing from its soybean processing containment basin. Hexane is as explosive as natural gas, when mixed with the right amount of air. In defending the case, John McCall hired an expert who produced a simulation video of how the containment basin was overflowing with hexane, spilling into the sewer, running miles downstream. After mixing with air to become an explosive blend, it ignited and caused the catastrophic event. The car crossing the manhole above contacted the fumes and ignition occurred. The video was dramatic evidence, indeed. My law partner briefed and argued for its admissibility at trial. On the eve of trial, U.S. District Court Judge Thomas Ballantine agreed to admit into evidence a computer simulation video for the first time in a Federal Court. That video caused Ralston Purina's defense to collapse; they settled without a trial. Ralston Purina paid approximately $33 million dollars in damages to a variety of parties including the Metropolitan Sewer District. The three defendants we represented were each dismissed. My Mass Tort career began with success.

ENGLISH AND AMERICAN COMMON LAW

Before we address the errors and wrongs in the U.S. civil justice system, you should have a basic understanding of how our litigation evolved over a long period. At the time of writing our Constitution, an English system of legal justice was already in place in America. As you know, prior to the Revolutionary War, we were a British colony. Thomas Jefferson is attributed with authoring much of our own U.S. Constitution. Jefferson, as well as the other 31 Founding Fathers that were also lawyers, were familiar with the English system as it existed in their new country. So, much of the English system was embraced by them and can still be found in the U.S. legal system.

England has a "common law" legal system, meaning that in order to determine whether a wrong has occurred justifying a lawsuit, a lawyer must read and interpret prior published case law decisions. If the lawyer can find a justification in the law books, he is good to go. In essence, the written decisions by appellate courts over the years constitute legal precedents. These legal precedents become the "law of the land." This British system was copied by America in 1778. We and England are not the only countries with a common law system; other countries founded with this legal system are Ireland, Scotland, Australia, and New Zealand.

However, the common law system is not the only legal system. For instance, France, Germany, and Italy have "civil law" systems derived from Roman law.[1] They have large books of codes which constitute the law of the land. To determine if the basis for a lawsuit exists, you must look it up

---

[1] Civil Law (legal system), New World Encyclopedia (February 23, 2017). Retrieved from http://www.newworldencyclopedia.org/entry/Civil_law_(legal_system).

in a code book. This book does not examine these countries or their legal system.

Additionally, it does not address or touch upon criminal law — an entirely different problem of its own. While there may be valid criticism of the American criminal justice system for imprisoning more persons by far than any other country, that was not my area of law practice. In fact, the word "crime" rarely appears in this book. Like code law, crimes are violations of statutes, not of common law cases.

The term "civil" has two meanings within the law. In civil code countries, it refers to the books containing the law of the land. In common law countries, it refers to all law that is not criminal. In England and America "civil" refers to our "common law" system of decided cases. This is known as *stare decisis* to lawyers, meaning the system of laws based on prior case decisions. The published decisions of appellate courts, both Federal and State, constitute this common law.

In our trial courts, the person filing the lawsuit is a "Plaintiff" and whoever he sues is a "Defendant." At the end of a jury trial there is a winner and a loser. After a judgment is entered, if the losing lawyer believes the judge made errors, he can appeal to an Appellate Court, which is a Court of Appeals. In the Federal courts as many as a dozen judges sit on the Court of Appeals in every state. Usually, a three-judge panel will read the losing lawyer's brief, and the opposing briefs, and hear the lawyers' oral arguments. The three judges decide the case by either affirming the lower court so the jury decision stands or overruling the trial judge, sending the case back for another trial. The loser at this level can then petition the entire Court to review the three-judge decision. After more legal briefs and oral arguments, if he loses a second time, he can petition the U.S. Supreme Court to take his case. However, the Supreme Court only accepts a small number of appealed cases, ones which they believe are significant and worthy of their time. The states have similar trial courts and Appellate

Court systems. Often, an Appellate Court publishes a written decision. It becomes the law of the land, *stare decisis*.

There are thousands upon thousands of law books containing these published opinions. New opinions are written and published daily. Thus, the civil common law is living, breathing and growing every day in our courts.

This book is based on only a part of our common law system of justice, specifically on the area of Tort law and jury trials. A "Tort" is a civil wrong that results in injury to another or his property.[2] The most common Torts are claims of negligence, product liability, malpractice, trespass and defamation or libel. If the claim becomes a lawsuit, then it may result in a jury trial. A trial is presided over by a judge, with the questions of fact decided by a jury who are the ultimate decisionmakers. Questions of fact require the jury to weigh the strength of the evidence and credibility of the witnesses. For example, who ran a red light or was a product defectively made? Although some of the Tort claims involve statutes, most are common law, meaning they derive from custom and judicial precedent. If the jury finds fault and liability, then it also determines the amount of damages to be paid to the harmed party.

The standard of "reasonable care" that defines negligence is the largest and best example of a Tort. If a driver runs a red light causing a collision, the legal standard of observing and stopping for a red light is a statute. A statute is a written law passed by a legislative body. The statute defines "reasonable care" that should be exercised by an individual at the traffic intersection. Similarly, if a person is chopping down a tree and it falls on a neighboring property producing an injury and damages, the question is would a reasonable person using ordinary care cut down the tree in that manner. Here, cases of prior tree cuttings would be relevant in deciding whether or

---

[2] Tort, Wex Legal Dictionary. Retrieved from https://www.law.cornell.edu/wex/tort

not reasonable care was taken. Moreover, because the tree fell into the neighbor's yard, a second tort claim could be made for trespass. Lastly, if a company sells a product that injures someone, there may be a product liability claim. Product liability refers to the liability of the manufacturer or seller for the injuries or damages caused by its allegedly defective product. Was the product made with reasonable care to avoid any defect? Look for a case like it—*stare decisis*.

When the Founding Fathers were writing the United States Constitution in 1787, there was already an existing body of common law that had migrated with them to the United States from England. Thirty-two of the 55 framers of the Constitution were lawyers; thus, they were familiar with this common law already.[3] Therefore, other than the laws recited in the Constitution, the "inalienable rights," they saw no need to spend time writing statutes. If your cattle escaped and damaged your neighbor's property, or you drove your wagon recklessly and caused a collision, the law was already established by *stare decisis*. The American common law grew from there, parallel to the common law of England. A Tort in England was a Tort in America and *vice versa*.

[3] How Many of the Founding Fathers Were Lawyers? State Bar of Michigan Blog (July 04, 2011). Retrieved from https://sbmblog.typepad.com/sbm-blog/2011/07/how-many-of-the-founding-fathers-were-lawyers.html.

THE ROOTS OF THE PROBLEM

When drafting the U.S. Constitution, our Founders relied heavily on the British civil justice system. They adopted most of the system, but not one important part of it. (You will see the trouble this seemingly innocent mistake on their part has made, in a later chapter.) Over the following 200 years, the U.S. court system worked well. But then, U.S. lawyers, aided by judges, began to tamper with it — to their benefit.

There are six areas of civil law where the lawyers helped themselves. These six legal aberrations are *unique to the United States*. No other country has chosen to either adopt or follow them. Here is a brief fly-over of these six aberrations, which I will explain in detail in later chapters.

First, is the *unique American Rule versus the English Rule* regarding the *payment of attorney fees*. In America, if you win your case, you still pay your own lawyer's fee, which is often a huge expense. To the contrary, the English Rule *requires the loser to pay the lawyer's fee of the winner*. This has a chilling effect on both meritless litigation and defenses. If you lose, you must pay *both* lawyers. The English Rule is the rule in all world-wide democracies, including Canada — *except the U.S.*

Second, is the existence of *contingency fee arrangements*, which permits a lawyer to own a large percentage of the plaintiff's claim for damages. For instance, if the plaintiff wins and collects $100,000, he only gets $60,000 because his lawyer gets $40,000 as his fee. This rule of law has been present in the U.S. for decades; it contributes to the explosion of unnecessary litigation. This rule has not existed elsewhere until recently, but even then, such fees are permitted only in limited circumstances and subject to strict regulations. *Not so in the United States*.

Third, is the Constitutional rule that a "*jury of citizens*" will decide both *fact issues* and the *damages* in a civil trial. In the U.S., the judge decides only issues of law. In every other country, the law, fact issues and damages are all decided by a *learned judge.* A trial before a judge eliminates many of the problems that jury trials present. *No other country uses this jury system for facts and damages.*

Fourth, is the use of "*class actions*" in a *wide variety of cases*. The Supreme Court governs class actions. A class action joins all identical claims together into a single lawsuit. In the U.S., they can be filed against anything, *e.g.*, producers of bird food, spam, candy, ginger ale, soap, massages, and many others. Lawyers receive large fees for filing them. In the area of Mass Tort law, they turn small claims into oppressive lawsuits with excessive lawyers' fees. *Class actions are uniquely codified in the U.S.*

Fifth, is the *right for lawyers to advertise.* This opened the door in the U.S. to both misinformation and the expansion of lawsuits. It has also undermined the professionalism and trust of lawyers. Lawyer ads are now seen everywhere. It is *prevalent only in the United States.*

Sixth, is *the political selection of judges in the U.S.* The Federal Judges are selected by the President and confirmed by the Senate. This is in sharp contrast to the selection of judges in England and other democracies. There, the quality of the prospective judge is the only consideration and politics play no role. In the U.S. *politics is the determining factor.*

Compounding these six aberrations, the insurance industry piled on by creating a huge source of litigation funding with "*cost of defense*" settlements. These occur because the bigger the lawsuit, the bigger the lawyer fees; so, the cost of defending this type of lawsuit can mushroom. If the insured wins, his lawyer's fee must still be paid by it. So, the insurance company will pay a settlement to close its file, even if the defenses are sound. The insurance company simply decides that the suit is costing too much. This practice has sponsored questionable lawsuits to obtain these settlements and driven up the cost of defending large lawsuits.

Added to all of this is the *expansion in the number of lawyers in America*. One writer suggests that America has 80 percent of the lawyers in the world with only four percent of the population. Think about that! The U.S. has *four times as many lawyers as the other democratic countries added together*. Is the U.S. a "nation of lawyers"? Moreover, law schools are producing about 40,000 new lawyers each year.

Further on are the chapters detailing historically how each aberration occurred. Collectively, they have created a legal system that favors lawyers at a high cost to you and the citizenry. The U.S. Supreme Court created many of these problems with myopic, erroneous decisions. Today, the Justices sit idly by as all of this occurs. How do the aberrations play out in the real world? The examples of my major lawsuits that follow will tell the tale.

To give you more insight and further your legal education, I will review with you what I believe are the two most important aberrations that have negatively impacted the civil justice system. They both involve the payment of lawyers' fees, which are often a major part of litigation expense. Thus, they are critical to the initial decision whether to file a lawsuit at all.

The first aberration refers to the English Rule versus the American Rule, which I mentioned briefly. Recall that under the American Rule the loser pays nothing when he loses, although he sued wrongfully. The second aberration is contingency fees, where the lawyer owns an interest, often 40%, in his client's lawsuit recovery. You will see how this ownership fee arrangement drives large lawsuits and often deceives the lawyer's client.

"ENGLISH RULE": LOSER PAYS ATTORNEY FEES

The English Rule allowing defendants to recover their attorney's fees when they win lawsuits can be traced back a long time. In 1875, the Rules of Court adopted the common law and granted English judges the ability to award lawyer's fees as costs to the winning party.[4] This has been the law of England for more than a century and a half. Throughout the long history of the English common law justice system the "English Rule" has applied. Stated simply, under the "English Rule," at the conclusion of any civil lawsuit, unless otherwise provided by statute or contract, the loser must pay the winner's lawyer's fees. The rationale for this rule is that the litigants are entitled to legal representation and should not have to bear the cost of either bringing a successful claim or successfully defending against a claim.

If the plaintiff files a meritless lawsuit, he runs the risk of having to pay the defendant's attorney's fees if the suit is dismissed. So, there is a substantial, potential risk of loss when he decides to sue. On the other hand, if the defendant is at fault, defends and then loses the lawsuit, he must pay for both the damage he caused plus the entire cost of the litigation, including both lawyers' fees. If he knows he is guilty of a civil wrong, he has a big risk when he decides to defend against a valid lawsuit. The "English Rule" provides a significant disincentive for asserting meritless claims or asserting baseless defenses. In England, litigation is serious business, indeed.

With one exception, every democratic country has adopted

---

[4] John F. Vargo, The American Rule on Attorney Fee Allocation: The Injured Person's Access to Justice, 42 AMERICAN UNIVERSITY L. REV. 1571 (1993).

the "English Rule." *The United States is that exception.* To the contrary, other than Alaska[5], the United States has its own "American Rule." To say the "American Rule" encourages lawsuit filings — especially those without merit — is a colossal understatement. How did this happen?

At the time of the U.S. Constitution, litigation in America was quite limited, focused mainly on the Chancery Courts and Admiralty Courts. Tort lawsuits were largely non-existent. In both Chancery (usually real property and collection disputes) and Admiralty (losses caused at sea) cases, the court awarded "costs" to the winner. The "costs" often included the loser's payment of attorney fees to the winner. This continued throughout the 18th century with various legislative enactments at both the state level and in the U.S. Congress. The end of 18th century reversed this issue in 1796, when the U.S. Supreme Court established the "American Rule" in *Arcambel v. Wiseman.*[6] The Court overruled the award of a $1,600 attorney fee in the case to be paid by the loser. Then in 1851, 55 years later, the Court affirmed the *Arcambel* decision by holding that a jury *cannot* include an attorney's fee as part of awarding damages.

Finally, in 1853, Congress entertained the issue by deciding that the winning party may only collect docket fees, between $5-$20; attorneys' fees were excluded.[7] This Act, known as the "Fee Bill," still exists today. Thus, the remnants of the English Rule disappeared 166 years ago, replaced by the unique American Rule requiring each party in a U.S. lawsuit to pay his own attorney's fee.

Much has been written on both sides of this issue by legal scholars over the past 100 years. Lengthy arguments are

---

[5] AS 09.60.010

[6] Arcambel v. Wiseman, 3 U.S. 306 (1796).

[7] Act of February 26, 1853, ch. 80, 10 State. 161 (Codified as amended at 28 U.S.C. 1920, 1923(a) (1988).

presented supporting each Rule. For the purposes of the issues presented in my book, the American Rule plays a dominant role. Agree with it or not, the U.S. Supreme Court summed up the application for using the American Rule in the U.S. in *Fleishman Distilling Corp. v. Maier Brewing Co.*:

> "[S]ince litigation is at best uncertain one should not be penalized for merely defending or prosecuting a lawsuit, and that the poor might be unjustly discouraged from instituting actions to vindicate their rights if the penalty for losing included the fees of their opponents' counsel..."[8]

Thus, it is the law of the land. The extensive harm it causes marches on in a nation of lawyers.

[8] Fleishman Distilling Corp. v. Maier Brewing Co., 386 U.S. 714 (1967).

CONTINGENCY FEES AND THE IMPORTANCE OF CHAMPERTY

In England, court-administered civil justice places its emphasis on greater accessibility and decreased cost and complexity. The English legal system recognized early the need for its legal counselors, Solicitors (the practicing lawyers) and Barristers (the trial lawyers) to maintain a high degree of professionalism. Lawyers are retained by clients to provide a high standard of ethical legal advice. They owe 100 percent of their loyalty to representing only their client's interest. This was a bedrock foundation for an exceptional system of justice. This concept is as old as the Magna Carta. Thus, "champerty" was adopted as the law of the land. Champerty made it illegal for a person with no previous interest in a lawsuit to finance it with the hopes of receiving a share of the profits if the suit succeeds[9]. It was not only unprofessional, but also illegal, for the lawyer to own any interest in his client's case. Such an ownership would dilute his duty of fealty to only his client, as his own interests could conflict with that of his client's. Champerty laws are also in place to prevent meritless and wrongful claims financed by others.

Originally, champerty was both a crime and a tort. However, this was abolished in 1967.[10] Today, English legislation permits an agreement for a prospective plaintiff to make his lawyer's contingency fee payable only in certain circumstances — as long as it complies with specified

---

[9] *See*, Champerty, Oxford dictionary.

[10] Andrew Evans and Nicholas Thompsell, Funding Litigation—the good, the bad and the ugly, Fieldfisher (July 28, 2016). Retrieved from https://www.fieldfisher.com/publications/2016/07/funding-litigation-the-good-the-bad-and-the-ugly.

regulations.[11] Therefore, these sort of financing agreements between client and attorney, referred to as conditional fee agreements, are permitted in limited circumstances. Absent these limited circumstances, the common law against champerty still exists. In general, a contract for funding of litigation will be unenforceable on champerty grounds if it is contrary to public policy, illegal, or improper. For example, a court takes into consideration the amount of profit the funder stands to make.

When the American legal system began, champerty was imbedded in it as well. This persisted for nearly 200 years. All lawyers in the United States who practiced law, including litigation, were paid by the hour or by a predetermined contractual amount. They were like plumbers. They kept time sheets and submitted bills to their clients either monthly or at the end of the case. Their hourly rates could vary widely, based primarily on two factors: geographic location and experience. In big cities like New York, Chicago and Los Angeles fees were much higher versus smaller cities and towns. Further, years of practice and more experience allegedly produced better lawyers and allowed for higher hourly fees to be charged. The differences in hourly rates can be large. Some experienced defense lawyers in big cities today can earn more than $1,500 per hour. Young small-town lawyers may charge only 10% of that amount. After hundreds of years, this hourly billing system was to change for plaintiff lawyers but not for defense lawyers. They continue to remain locked into hourly billing for the foreseeable future, although there are now some lump sum fee defense contracts.

In the 1950s, academics and lawyers criticized champerty in favor of a rule that a lawyer should be able to represent his

---

[11] *See* Courts and Legal Services Act of 1990 (CLSA) §58- 58A, available at https://www.fakongjian.com/int_doc/laws/20160603/2241/gb263en20160603224106.pdf (pgs. 39-40).

client for a fee based on a percentage of the recovery he obtains for the client's claim. This became known as a lawyer's "contingency fee" contract. Its subsequent approval by the courts spread like wildfire through the American legal system. America became the only country with open, unrestricted contingency fees.

It is now a dominant attorney/client contract in Tort cases. It has also expanded to patent, contract, anti-trust and similar non-Tort lawsuits. The contingency fee contract is the currency today for plaintiff's lawyers. It can result in upwards of 40 percent of the damages awarded at trial (or the amount received in a settlement) going to the attorney for fees and expenses. The contingency fee contracts explain why in cities and towns across the country, plaintiff's lawyers are some of the wealthiest citizens. But make no mistake, some of these lawyers are excellent and persuasive trial attorneys.

When looking at contingency fees, consider three cases as examples. In the 2018 case in St. Louis, Johnson & Johnson lost the jury trial involving the ingredients found in baby powder. After a five-week trial, the jury awarded the plaintiffs damages in the amount of $4.6 billion. The contingency fee lawyer made $1.5 billion for himself if he can collect on this verdict. Not bad for a few months of work! In the Monsanto case, tried in San Francisco, the jury awarded the plaintiff $289 million. If his lawyer gets a 40 percent contingency fee, he earns $115 million. Again, not a bad payment for a few months' work! In the same year, in New York City, a woman pulled a Cybex exercise machine onto herself when she failed to use equipment properly while she was stretching. The injury, caused by her misuse, left her partially paralyzed. She received $66 million from the jury — $23 million for her lawyers. Good work...indeed

Another recent Mass Tort case illustrates just how outrageous a continency fee can be. In 2018, many females brought lawsuits against manufacturers of pelvic mesh implants for problems allegedly caused by their treatment with pelvic mesh. Regarding these pelvic mesh cases, a *New York Times* article stated:

> *Litigation over pelvic mesh, also called transvaginal mesh, ranks as one of the biggest mass tort cases in United States history, in terms of claims filed, number of corporate defendants and settlement dollars. Seven medical device manufacturers, including Boston Scientific and Johnson & Johnson, are paying nearly $8 billion to resolve the claims of more than 100,000 women*[12].

In one of these cases, Plaintiff Sherise Grant received a settlement of $12,000 for the damages caused by the side effects of her pelvic mesh implant. After attorney fees, her payout was a mere $3,500 — not even enough to cover the cost of removal of her pelvic mesh implant. In addition to the inclusion of meals and hotels as part of the attorney's fee, her contingency fee agreement allowed for the cost of travel by private plane. In another pelvic mesh case, Plaintiff Michelle Hedgcoth received a settlement of $140,000, which is on the high end of pelvic mesh settlements. The implant and its removal left her with permanent injuries, as parts of the mesh became embedded in her body. After attorneys' fees and expenses, she took home only $50,000. Cases like these show the abuses of continency fees in the United States.

There are arguments both supporting and opposing continency fees. Supporters argue that continency fees allow equal access to the courts. A poor but injured plaintiff lacks the financial resources to sue and challenge a large corporation

---

[12] Matthew Goldstein, As Pelvic Mesh Settlements Near $8 Billion, Women Question Lawyers' Fees, New York Times (Feburary 1, 2019). Retrieved from https://www.nytimes.com/2019/02/01/business/pelvic-mesh-settlements-lawyers.html.

with its financial resources, large insurance policies and choice of lawyers. Simply put, it is not a fair fight.

On the other hand, contingency fee cases are ripe for abuse and a growing number of abuses are occurring. The major criticism is that the lawyer can control the lawsuit with his interest foremost and not that of his client. His primary obligation to his client is thus compromised. Should I settle or should I go to trial and risk receiving nothing? The position of a rich lawyer and a poor client places this choice in opposition.

A third criticism of continency fees is that such contracts sponsor more litigation, a whole lot more. This criticism has proven true. There has been an explosion of civil litigation in the U.S. In 1970, 87,321 civil lawsuits were filed in the U.S.[13] This is compared to the 277,010 in 2018.[14] Moreover, in Chief Justice John Roberts 2021 Year End Report on the Federal Judiciary, which he delivered to the U.S. Congress, he cites the *Wall Street Journal* reported data that 2.5 million civil lawsuits were filed between 2000 and 2018. This dramatic increase does not count the tens of thousands of civil lawsuits filed in the state courts each year.

Recently, wealthy hedge funds searching for less risky investment opportunities have entered the market in concert with plaintiff's law firms. Together, they have determined that the financial return for making loans to plaintiffs, and also recovering part of settlements with a contingent fee, are superior to other investments. According to the *New York*

---

[13] Jürgen O, Skoppek, B. The Growth of Litigation, Mackinac Center for Public Policy (July 1, 1989). Retrieved from available at https://www.mackinac.org/6263.

[14] Federal Judicial Caseload Statistics 2018, United States Court. Retrieved from https://www.uscourts.gov/statistics-reports/federal-judicial-caseload-statistics-2018.

Times, litigation finance is at least a $10 billion industry[15]. Historically, this investment in a lawsuit was prohibited, but not anymore. The ideal that the client is paramount in the lawyer's mind is undermined by the lawyer's or third-party's stake in the outcome.

Another New York Times article highlights the problems caused by the involvement of third parties in litigation finance[16]. Investors are not only investing in pending lawsuits, but also creating these lawsuits with the help of marketing firms who seek out potential plaintiffs. A Brooklyn prosecutor is investigating a network of plaintiff's lawyers, finance firms, and others. They may have induced women to seek the unnecessary removal of their pelvic mesh implants in order to improve their chances of obtaining large lawsuit settlements. In particular, these financing companies offer clients high interest loans — sometimes 50 percent — that have to be repaid if the client receives an award from the case. "Interviews with dozens of women, lawyers, finance executives, and marketers, as well as a review of court records and confidential documents, indicate that hundreds, perhaps thousands, of women have been sucked into this assembly-line-like system."[17]

Contingency fees are deceiving the people they were intended to benefit. They are often the losers while the lawyers — and others in cahoots with them — are the winners.

---

[15] Matthew Goldstein and Jessica Silver-Greenberg, Hedge Funds Look to Profit From Personal-Injury Suits, The New York Times (June 25, 2018). Retrieved from https://www.nytimes.com/2018/06/25/business/hedge-funds-mass-torts-litigation-finance.html.

[16] *Id.*

[17] *id.*

JURY TRIALS MUST BE "JUST, SPEEDY AND INEXPENSIVE"

Before beginning this historical journey across my Mass Tort litigation, you must always keep in mind a promise made in 1937 by the U.S. Supreme Court. The Supreme Court manages and controls all the litigation and proceedings in all the Federal Courts. More than eight decades ago, the Supreme Court set the standard for all Federal Court litigation in its Federal Rules of Civil Procedure, Rule #1. Every lawsuit filed in every Federal Court must follow this Rule. In that Rule, the Supreme Court boldly states: "*it is the purpose of the courts in the U.S. to secure the just, speedy, and inexpensive determination of every action and proceeding.*" (Emphasis added) So, remember when reading my cases, the Supreme Court has directed that every lawsuit must be "*just, speedy and inexpensive*"! This is the law of the land for lawyers to follow.

BEVERLY HILLS SUPPER CLUB (1977)

To demonstrate how these six aberrations and flaws affect real life litigation, I start with the Beverly Hills Supper Club fire. It became one the first Mass Tort lawsuits in the U.S.

The Supper Club was a Las Vegas-style dinner club in northern Kentucky, less than two and a half miles across the Ohio river from Cincinnati. It booked top-notch entertainment and catered to the affluent. On the night of May 28, 1977, the Cabaret Room of the Supper Club was packed to excess with patrons for the headlining act and popular singer of the time, John Davidson.

As the plates were being cleared and preparations for the main show began, a fire of unknown origin broke out in a room down the hall. The room contained stored furniture. When the furniture ignited, the room quickly filled with smoke and then flames. The staff attempted to extinguish the fire without alerting the patrons. They failed. The fire grew and penetrated into the hallway leading to the Cabaret Room. In the hall it gained fresh oxygen and fuel. Meanwhile, there were no sprinklers in the building to contain the fire or alarms to alert those in the building. The carpeting, wood paneling, ceiling tiles, side tables and chairs began to overheat and then they ignited. The fire gained strength and speed as it rolled down the length of the hall toward the Cabaret Room. The entire building was defenseless, as were its inhabitants. A major tragedy was now unavoidable.

In the Cabaret Room, anticipation for the show was building as the opening comics, Teter and McDonald, were performing. A busboy, Walter Bailey, came on stage and interrupted the comics to announce the fire, but few patrons responded initially. The lights in the building flickered and a melee ensued as nearly a thousand guests scrambled for the exits. Many of the exits were disguised, which is common in nightclubs, or locked to prevent non-paying guests from entering the room. The locked and disguised exits soon became jammed with bodies. At the end of the ghastly night, 165 patrons were dead, hundreds more hospitalized and countless others were traumatized.

After the Supper Club fire, Cincinnati and Northern Kentucky were staring at a tragedy of unmeasurable proportions. However, one man's disaster is often another man's opportunity. After the ashes at the Supper Club cooled, plaintiff's lawyers congregated, and the lawsuits began.

The Supper Club was without adequate insurance and assets to pay these enormous claims. Thus, began what would become one of the first Mass Tort lawsuits. As before stated, a "mass tort" designates a lawsuit(s) for a large number of injuries and/or deaths caused by a single event, *e.g.* a plane crash or fire disaster, or by a product, *e.g.* asbestos or pharmaceuticals that cause injury to thousands of users. It often carries with it special procedures crafted to handle large scale litigation with many plaintiffs and many defendants. The Supper Club lawsuits were filed — by hundreds of plaintiffs — against more than 130 defendants who allegedly had some manner of "contact" to the Supper Club or its furnishings. An Ohio Federal Judge was assigned the case. He sat in conjunction with the local Kentucky Circuit Judge in a parallel lawsuit. The lawsuits — with four lengthy jury trials and appeals — consumed seven years. *See*, *In re Beverly Hills Supper Club Fire Litigation*, 639 F. Supp. 915 (E.D. Ky, 1981). It would spawn more mass tort cases and prove to exemplify that America is, indeed, a "nation of lawyers."

The Federal judge, Carl Rubin, took control of the proceedings as it grew in size and complexity. Unfortunately, this new judge had little experience with jury trials, product liability lawsuits or negligence claims. I was told he had been a real estate and estate lawyer, and Ohio Senator Robert Taft's campaign manager. His appointment to a Federal judgeship illustrates the potential problem of inexperienced, political appointments. He got the case because apparently no experienced sitting federal judge wanted it.

A creative Cincinnati plaintiff's lawyer, Stanley Chesley, together with others, created this massive litigation. He faced what should have been serious obstacles. The Supper Club was a fire disaster waiting to happen with a litany of fire code violations. These included no sprinklers, no fire safety training, no fire alarms, hidden exits, locked exits, a failure to promptly warn the patrons, and gross over-crowding. The Supper Club was the obvious cause of the deaths and injuries. That said however, it did not have the resources for a large payout, so the plaintiff's lawyers convinced the judge to indulge in their scheme to go after bigger fish. The judge also ignored my oral argument and certified the case as a "class action" binding together all the plaintiffs' claims.

The precise cause of the fire in the room down the hall was never known. This is not uncommon in fires that do not involve arson. A fire destroys what is burning. In a building that has a fully engaged fire, the fire is burning and destroying the evidence of where and how it started. As a result, many fires of unknown origin are automatically blamed by fire departments on electrical wiring. This is an easy scapegoat because faulty electrical connections can cause fires and electrical connections are prevalent in every building.

Transporting electricity over a small wire requires a metal that is a good conductor. Gold is the best conductor, but it has far more value in jewelry and as a commodity than as wire. Moreover, all the gold electrical wire would be stolen! As a result, most of the electrical wire is made of copper. Nevertheless, aluminum, while not as good a conductor as copper, is much cheaper and is adequate for shorter distances, as in housing and appliances. The aluminum industry entered the wire market in 1965. It is no longer in the market.

The plaintiff's lawyers devised a claim that aluminum electrical wire was present in a room wall socket where the fire began. Further, the aluminum wire was attached to an electrical plug with copper screws. This, in turn, can allegedly cause "creep" to occur between the different metals because they do not join readily. When the alleged creep creates a gap, a spark can occur. When a spark occurs, if a flammable product is nearby, a fire is possible. Judge Rubin, wanting this big case in his court to move forward, recognized the alleged claim.

Some things in the law should be self-evident. It is not always so. For example, if a person suffers an injury, he or she must identify and name the person, or product manufacturer, who caused the injury. This is unchallenged law, both criminal and civil. The television crime shows are replete with arrested and accused bad actors pleading the "alibi" defense: "I was not at the crime scene; I was home in bed." So it is also in civil cases.

In the Supper Club fire, the plaintiffs' attorneys alleged the fire was started by defective aluminum wire creep. They believed there could have been as much as six miles of cheap aluminum wire used in the Supper Club building and therefore it started the fire. Who manufactured the aluminum wire for them to sue?

Fires destroy evidence. Aluminum wire, the cheaper wire, burns up at 1221 degrees Fahrenheit. Copper wire, the better wire, burns at 1981 degrees Fahrenheit. A normal fire can burn at 1600 degrees Fahrenheit. The fire consumed the aluminum wire. The copper plug used at the alleged socket where the alleged creep occurred was still there, but the aluminum wire was gone. There is no specific aluminum wire company to identify or name in a suit.

No problem for the plaintiff's lawyers. They will sue all the companies. They will apply to newly appointed Judge Rubin to create a new unprecedented claim. Let us call it "Enterprise Liability" and dispense with the existing law. A suit was drawn up and filed against all the aluminum wire manufacturers the lawyers could find. That included more than a dozen defendants. Some were large companies like Alcoa, Reynolds Metals, South Wire and Anaconda. Others were small companies. Because aluminum wire was also made as far away as China, some could not be sued at all. They were cooking up an original lawsuit stew.

In a jury trial, the plaintiff has the "burden of proof." This means when the plaintiff's lawyer closes his case, he must have shown it is more likely than not that he should win. When you see a representation of Lady Justice, she is robed and blind folded. She is holding a scale. The plaintiff must prove that her scale is tilted in his favor. The defendant challenges the plaintiff's case with a motion to dismiss. If the judge decides the challenge in favor of the plaintiff, then the defense lawyer must present his case. But this time in the Supper Club case, the judge reversed the burden of proof. This was novel, indeed. Now the burden of proof will shift, as each new wire defendant must prove it was not its product in the Supper Club. All these defendants meant many new lawyers would come into the case. Instead of a small trial against an identified aluminum wire manufacturer as the defendant, whose product may have been the alleged cause of the creep and the fire, the multiplied defendants will make the trial enormously expensive to defend. Remember, lawyers like to congregate.

This single-issue trial with a reversed burden of proof — unheard of previously — would determine whether or not the "creep" caused the fire. All the fault of the Supper Club was set aside. A multi-week trial ensued, which was won by the defendants. But bad news followed the victory. After the trial, one of the jurors revealed that he had examined the aluminum wiring and copper plugs in his house. He found no creep. He reported this finding during jury deliberations. This personal test by a juror — not part of the evidence at the trial — was improper; it caused the verdict to be set aside and voided. A second aluminum wire trial would be — and was — held at a future date.

Having failed in their first effort, the Judge and the

plaintiff's lawyers devised a second novel trial. In this trial, it was assumed that the aluminum wire caused the fire, so its wire insulation could be a bad and toxic product and would be a fuel for the fire. This seems incredible on its face for a number of reasons. First, the insulation is made from polyvinyl chloride ("PVC"). PVC is a miracle product invented by the Germans in the 1940s. It is the vinyl you see everywhere as wire insulation, chair covers, raincoats, on car seats, tablecloths, etc. — it is ever present in our lives. Moreover, it lasts nearly forever, it is water repellent, very plastic or malleable. It is difficult to ignite or burn unless thrown into a fire. To argue it is unreasonably dangerous defies logic. Further, the PVC wire insulation does not burn with a flame if you put a match to it. Nevertheless, the Judge devised a product liability trial for PVC: is PVC wire insulation unreasonably dangerous? Because the wire company that used the wire insulation could not be found, the entire PVC industry was sued. Once again, only passing reference could be made to the true cause of the tragedy, the Supper Club.

I participated in this trial as a lead defense counsel representing two large and well-known companies, U.S. Steel and Firestone. They happened to make PVC. Other large tire, oil and petrochemical companies were also PVC producers, so they were sued and brought into the case, including General Electric, BFGoodrich, Goodyear, Tenneco, Diamond Shamrock, Occidental Petroleum, and others. They all appeared in Judge Rubin's courtroom with lawyers in tow. Extensive discovery and long expert witness depositions ensued prior to setting a trial date.

Before the trial, the defendants held meetings to decide what to do about the pending trial and the first Mass Tort case that appeared as if it could go on forever. Another aluminum wire trial would be held, as would one for the furnishings. In fact, seven years were consumed in the litigation; simply stated, the litigation was beyond enormous — and this was the 1970s.

There were two opposing camps at the meetings. One group believed they should settle the case on the basis of the cost of defense, which was proving ever larger. Further, if they lost this weird trial, they could be looking at more trials and ultimately a huge damage claim for all the deaths and injuries caused by the fire. The other group believed that this entire case was bogus and simply "blackmail." Their concern was that since PVC wire insulation is used everywhere, they could be sued in every future fire. Thus, they would try the case and defend their product. My clients chose to defend the case.

I went to trial with a group of about a dozen excellent defense lawyers. It was truly a strange and unprecedented proceeding. The claim was based on PVC's alleged fire performance, but the Supper Club fault for the fire disaster could not be directly referenced. Some of the testimony was bizarre. For instance, the plaintiffs presented a woman, we will call her "Debra," as an expert witness. She had an obscure PhD in toxicology — her thesis involved sea mollusks in the Hudson River. Nevertheless, she concluded that fumes from PVC were especially toxic. In point of fact, PVC smoke *is* toxic; everything, both in nature and made by man, is toxic when burned. Never breathe smoke from a fire. One of the worst to burn is cabbage. It produces hydrogen cyanide, a gas used by the Germans in their death camps.

She claimed PVC was so toxic that all PVC should be banned — which was nonsense. To support her testimony, she videotaped an experiment she designed and conducted. She obtained some PVC pipe and, with her husband as an assistant, fired up their charcoal grill in their backyard. Their plan was to record the toxicity of the fire-produced PVC off-gases from roasting the pipe. To protect themselves they both wore complete scuba apparatus including masks. So here they were, in the open-air backyard, trying to burn a PVC pipe that was basically not flammable, only smoldering. Meanwhile, the tape was recording the heavy breathing from their scuba tanks. Bizarre indeed. Nevertheless, she testified PVC was unreasonably toxic, so her testimony created a potential fact issue for the jury to decide.

To make the description of a nine-week trial brief, at the end of the testimony Judge Rubin gave two instructions to the jury as the fact finder. First, is PVC wire insulation unreasonably dangerous? Second, did the PVC producers issue warnings about the toxicity of their product?

After a two-day deliberation, the jury returned a verdict. *PVC wire insulation is not unreasonably dangerous! We won the trial!* The result was what it should be. However, they also found the PVC defendants had not issued any warning. This was also true. The plaintiff's lawyers then averred that they had won also. This was more nonsense. Product liability law clearly states that if your product has an unreasonable danger, you can overcome the risk created by the danger with adequate warnings. A can of rat poisoning has a warning label. Rat poison is also poisonous to humans, so you must put a warning on the label. So, the second warning question requires a condition precedent finding on the first question that the product is dangerous. If there is no danger, there is nothing to warn about. There was no danger found by the jury. This dichotomy appeared lost on the trial judge at the time.

At this stage, our defense had prevailed on the safe product issue, so our clients were vindicated. At the same time the Judge appeared to be misunderstanding the warning verdict. He could then decide to create, from more whole cloth, yet another weird trial about its use when the fire occurred. Moreover, the second aluminum wire trial and the furnishings trial loomed in the near and distant future. The case could go on for years, which it did. It was time for cost of defense settlements! We all settled. Lawyers are expensive and the litigation was so large, unusual and excessive that it was better to stop the costs and settle out. Meanwhile, some of the aluminum wire companies had seen enough and settled also — for their cost of defense. The plaintiff's lawyers now possessed a cost of defense settlement war chest of millions of dollars because they sued so many defendants. It was extracted from dozens of defendants, all of whom had won their two jury trials, finding they were not at fault.

In fact, two more trials were held over the ensuing years! More defense cost settlements also occurred. Although I do not know the exact numbers because my defense work was concluded, I would guess that about $25 million was recovered in all. At a third for the lawyers, their fees were over $8 million. Quite a sum in the 1980s.

Which of the six aberrations of our civil law system played roles in the Supper Club litigation?

First, these civil trials were presented to juries of lay people, *i.e.* local citizens. A tragic disaster had occurred, so sympathies could run high, clouding otherwise good judgement. A "fair" jury for the defendants could be problematic. The trial presented complex issues of chemical analysis, physics, electrical engineering and safety, fire sciences, toxicology and understanding arcane fire codes. The jurors lacked specific expertise to make sense of it all. The aluminum wire creep experiment conducted at the juror's house in that trial demonstrates the problems he had in understanding the evidence in the trial. Even so, both the aluminum wire trial and the PVC trial were won by the defense. Had these claims been presented to a learned judge in England they would have been dismissed without the need for months of trials, years of litigation and millions of dollars in cost.

Second, the politically appointed judge in the case had little trial experience or a basic understanding of the legal issues involved. While he was a smart man, basically he got it wrong at each level... more than once. His inexperience was responsible for the large defense costs of the litigation. He was not a federal judge because of his trial experience and high standing. He was selected because of his political connections.

Third, the plaintiff's lawyers could expand the lawsuit as far as the judge would allow and that was quite far. When they lost in our trial, due to the American Rule they did not have to pay our substantial trial costs and attorney's fees. If the U.S. had the English Rule, I submit no lawsuit or trial would have occurred.

Fourth, the claims were based on contingency fees, so the more cost of defense settlements they could obtain, the richer they became. They created a huge cost of defense nightmare because it paid them handsomely, as much as $8 million.

Fifth, the plaintiffs did not win trials proving liabilities, then obtaining and collecting judgements. Their monies came from the cost of defense settlements paid by their insurers to buy their peace in this U.S. flawed justice system. It was simply too expensive to keep paying for such a large litigation.

Sixth, the judge ruled that the suit was a class action, even though each plaintiff's claim was different from every other depending on their location during the fire. By amalgamating all the claims, proving each single plaintiff's claim was avoided. This would have been a huge burden for the plaintiff's lawyers. In mass, they constituted a huge damage claim. This class action status also drove up cost of defense settlements. But in one respect, it also favored the defendants when they settled the case. A single settlement bound every plaintiff to it.

The Supper Club case model spawned 26 more years of mass disaster fire litigation cases. These included the Yonkers Department Store fire in 1981 in Des Moines, Iowa (ten deaths), the MGM Grand Hotel fire in Las Vegas, Nevada in 1983 (95 deaths), the San Juan DuPont Plaza Hotel fire, San Juan, Puerto Rico in 1988 (96 deaths), the Happy Land Social Club fire in Brooklyn, New York in 1990 (95 deaths) and The Station nightclub fire in Providence, Rhode Island in 2003 (100 deaths). They all involved litigation which mirrored, in many respects, each other. But what ended large hotel and building fires, and the Mass Tort lawsuits they caused, was the installation of sprinklers. Sprinklers diminish the fire safety risks in large buildings. I am not aware of any multiple deaths in a fully-operational sprinklered building fire.

The flaw of the American Rule makes large corporations hesitant to take cases to trial. Further, the abundance of available insurance increases the chance of buying peace by settling. However, some corporations fight back, not wanting to make themselves into targets for frivolous lawsuits. They make the lawyer earn his fee in a jury trial.

FINDING A DEFENSE – NEW YORK TELEPHONE AND YONKERS DEPARTMENT STORE

After the Supper Club trial concluded, I returned to my office in Louisville, Kentucky. Within a week I received a telephone call from the General Counsel of New York Telephone Company. New York Telephone owned an old, large concrete telephone exchange building on Sixth Avenue in the city. It was built in the 1920s and contained hundreds of miles of cable insulated with both earlier impregnated cloth and later PVC, along with thousands of switches. A mysterious fire had started in the underground vault. By the time the fire departments arrived, the fire was burning vigorously. There was an estimated ton of insulation on the wires. Over seven hundred firemen from seven fire departments fought the fire. They succeeded in protecting the surrounding buildings.

They fought the fire within the building until all their breathing cannisters were empty. It could not be extinguished. Ultimately, the fire burned out. It produced a huge plume of black smoke, visible in Boston. Over 200,000 phones in New York City went dead, including Wall Street. Many of the firemen were overcome from the acrid smoke but they all survived. One fireman, named Bresnan, had severe respiratory diseases. He was the poster child for a lawsuit; his father was a fireman, and his mother literally gave birth to him on the fire house floor. He retained an excellent New York City plaintiff's lawyer, Ivan Schneider. He sued New York Telephone, AT&T and Bell Laboratory for damages. He claimed, as in the Supper Club, that the PVC wire insulation was "unreasonably dangerous." If he won, many other firemen with smoke inhalation injuries could also present claims. Bresnan was the representative for all the injured firemen.

The three companies defended the case with an in-house New York Telephone Company trial attorney. Mr. Frank Natoli expected to have the suit dismissed, asserting the "fireman's rule" as a legal defense. That rule was the law of New York and elsewhere. It states that "firemen take the premises as they find them." All fires are dangerous, so firemen are trained in the necessary steps needed to protect themselves. That is why firemen injured while fighting fires do not file lawsuits. However, there is an exception to the rule in the case law. If unreasonably dangerous products are stored on the property when a fire occurs, the owner must give notice to the fire department so the firemen can protect themselves. For instance, if your home catches fire and you have 5,000 gallons of gasoline stored in the basement, tell the fire department. If the gasoline blows up in your house fire you are liable to any injured fireman. Bresnan's attorney argued that the enormous quantity of flammable PVC wire insulation stored in the vault and building was an unreasonably dangerous risk in a fire. New York Telephone should have advised and warned the fire department. Judge Greenberg agreed, overruling the motion for dismissal. He set the date for the jury trial in two weeks. New York Telephone was going to trial for a PVC fire without a trial defense in place.

The following Tuesday, I, my associate David Redmon, and my legal assistant, Cheri Dillard, flew to New York City. We met the attorneys at the New York Telephone Company skyscraper. We carried with us the defense of PVC we had presented successfully in the Supper Club fire case.

We set up offices in the New York Telephone building across from the courthouse at the foot of the Brooklyn Bridge. I joined the New York Telephone lawyer at the trial that began on Monday. My associate began interviewing New York City doctors and collecting Mr. Bresnan's medical records. My assistant organized our prior defense files, which were useful later.

In the third week of trial, Mr. Schneider called Dr. Victor

Esch to testify. Dr. Esch had a complete dossier on PVC smoke, its alleged harmfulness to humans and the effect of PVC smoke on firemen. He included pictures of the trachea of dead firemen. He would support the claim but he had not examined Mr. Bresnan.

Under New York law, expert witnesses are not deposed. You do not get to question the witness under oath before the trial. That is an old practice and follows the long-standing "trial by ambush" favored in New York. So, Mr. Schneider expected Dr. Esch to be a breeze because we were not permitted to question him about his opinions before trial. However, what he did not know was that Dr. Esch had testified in the Supper Club case. Therefore, I had both his trial testimony and his day long deposition under oath with me. We also had obtained the medical records of Mr. Bresnan. We had all the details of his injury and treatment. They were not consistent with, and did not confirm, PVC smoke exposure poisoning being testified to by Dr. Esch.

I cross-examined Dr. Esch that afternoon, taking him through his description of the telltale signs of a PVC smoke exposure. When he equivocated, he was confronted with his prior testimony under oath. I wrote his answers on a large poster chart in front of the jury. Of the nine symptoms he detailed, I knew only two were found in Mr. Bresnan's medical records. They could be explained away. Although Mr. Bresnan suffered serious smoke inhalation injuries, it could not be shown that they could be traced to PVC. They were caused by common carbon monoxide gas found in every fire. Ivan Schneider watched in silence. Toward the end of the day, Dr. Esch concluded and was dismissed.

Judge Greenberg had figured out what was happening with this lawyer from Kentucky. He excused the jurors and called all counsel into his chambers. He told Mr. Schneider, "This case has already taken too much of my time." He must settle it. Make an offer the defendants "cannot refuse." Then he told us not to refuse a fair offer. In essence, he believed we were winning the trial so it should be over.

The next day we came to Judge Greenberg's court to receive the offer (it is confidential). It was for less than our authority to settle, so we could accept it in chambers that morning. But I wanted to delay until later in the day because the next witness to be called for that day was Debra — the fish expert from the Supper Club trial discussed earlier — now magically a fire toxicologist expert witness. She was going to testify! I wanted the opportunity to cross-examine her on the record, plus I also had her prior trial and deposition testimony with me.

When we left chambers and entered the courtroom, we were shocked to see an EMS team. Mr. Bresnan had collapsed, was strapped to a stretcher and was going to the hospital. We immediately settled the lawsuit due to our concern with what effect that vision could have on jurors. No other firemen filed claims against New York Telephone. We returned to my law firm in Louisville, Kentucky.

Two months later I was at it again. A fire had occurred a year earlier in the Yonkers Department store in Des Moines, Iowa, killing ten employees on a Sunday morning. The two lawyers representing them visited Cincinnati to see parts of the Supper Club trial. They assumed the Yonkers fire was also electrical in origin — it was never determined exactly where or how it began — and sued the PVC industry in Des Moines. A similar group of PVC defendants were sued. They retained Des Moines attorneys. Tenneco retained me, and I retained Dick Smith, a terrific local defense lawyer. In fact, I will say that the quality of lawyering in Des Moines on all sides was high. Judge Jackson was experienced, thoughtful, respectful of attorneys and generally excellent. He was a pleasure to practice before.

I made many trips to Des Moines — trust me when I tell you the winters there are harsh — and lived in Des Moines from February until April of 1981 for the trial of the case. It was a single-issue trial. The trial involved only one question,

"Was the electrical wire and insulation the cause of the fire"? The trial turned out to be before one of the worst juries I have ever seen. The general community in Des Moines was educated and intelligent, but this jury was going to be problematic no matter what we did. Our chances did not look good.

Dick Smith and I made the opening statement for the defendants. In the Supper Club trial, I also made the opening statement. For that trial I had a jar of raw PVC. It looked like sugar. In describing why PVC was not dangerous, I opened the jar, took a spoon and swallowed some PVC. The courtroom was quiet. I had a long pause, then smiled and went on with the statement. No ill effects.

For this Yonkers trial I took a piece of insulated electrical wire and a Bic lighter. I burned it in front of the jury. The PVC would smolder and sizzle, but not produce a flame. When I removed the flame the PVC wire suddenly stopped smoking. How could this PVC wire insulation be the cause of the large fire in Yonkers?

After several unusual weeks, the jury returned a verdict for the plaintiffs, finding the fire's origin involved PVC. We defense lawyers were not surprised. So, our clients decided to go forward with cost of defense settlements which were reasonable considering the size of the case and single-issue trial. Only BFGoodrich was kept in the case for the next trial. BFGoodrich then retained me.

The plaintiffs' experts who testified at the trial had trouble starting the fire at the large electrical panel in Yonkers without showing an aberrant, and perhaps impossible, electrical overloading. I called it a cascading of electrical faults, which, even if true, no electrical wire insulation could withstand, not even PVC. Thus, the wire insulation performed as it should have. A superseding, intervening cascading electrical event overcame its inherent insulating abilities. Thus, no fault can be assigned to it. I filed post-trial motions for summary judgement on this basis. I argued the motion to Judge Strickland. He agreed and dismissed the case. We then settled BFGoodrich for less than the others, to avoid the cost of an appeal.

I had now successfully represented New York Telephone Company, U.S. Steel, Firestone, Tenneco and BFGoodrich. I had in my possession a complete PVC fire defense, tested in three trials. What could be next? It was the defense of the MGM Grand Hotel fire litigation. This was to become one of the largest Mass Tort litigations in U.S. history.

MGM GRAND HOTEL (1981)

On the morning of November 21, 1980, it was another normal day at the MGM Grand Hotel in Paradise (Las Vegas), Nevada. MGM Grand was the largest, and perhaps plushest, hotel in the world at that time — twenty-one stories high.[18] It was magnificent. The first floor contained an expansive and fancy casino, nearly one hundred yards long. At one end was a large grand and open lobby. At the other end was a small eatery called The Deli. There was no sprinkler system in The Deli to extinguish a fire. The Deli was exempted from the Las Vegas fire code requiring sprinklers because it was expected to be "occupied" twenty-four hours a day. The casino also had no sprinklers for the same reason. The code assumed people would be present to sound an alarm if a fire occurred in either room. On this fateful morning, The Deli was closed and empty.

Unbeknownst to anyone in the hotel, a fire — later believed to be of electrical arcing origin — was burning in The Deli. It was approximately seven o'clock in the morning and most of the five thousand guests were still asleep in their rooms.[19] The night before, they enjoyed excellent cocktails and dinners in one of the seven restaurants in the hotel, followed by a show or a night of gaming at the casino. They were totally unaware that the worst nightmare of their lives was about to occur.

---

[18] MGM Grand Hotel Fire Anniversary, Read the reports on what led up to this deadly fire and how firefighter's responder, Fire Rescue Magazine, (November 21, 2016). Retrieved from https://www.firerescuemagazine.com/articles/2016/11/mgm-grand-hotel-fire-anniversary.html

[19] *Id.*

Undetected, the fire grew, burning through the doors, entering the casino. In the casino was an array of plastic materials used in slot machines, gambling tables, coverings, mirrors, ornamentations, wood furniture, carpeting, wallpaper and other flammables just waiting to ignite and burn. And burn they did!

The investigation of the cause and effect of the fire by the Nevada Fire Marshall estimated that the casino fire raced through the length of the casino at fifteen to nineteen feet per second.[20] That is approximately the same speed of a good runner racing in a 100-yard dash. An average person in the casino that morning could not outrun this fire. Because it was only seven o'clock in the morning, just 18 died in the casino and lobby.[21]

After the fire grew rapidly in the casino, a huge fireball roared through the lobby and out the front doors. Numerous fire departments responded and fought the fire for the remainder of the day.[22] Thankfully, the fire could not spread to the upper floors of the hotel because sprinklers were in place. But the smoke did. [23]

The toxic smoke began penetrating the upper floors of the

---

[20] MGM Fire Investigation, Fire Scene Examination, Initial Response, Clark County Fire Department, V-17. Available at https://www.firerescuemagazine.com/content/dam/fe/downloads/FFN-FRM-Downloads-Editorial/MGM_FIRE.pdf

[21] MGM Grand Hotel Fire Anniversary, Read the reports on what led up to this deadly fire and how firefighter's responder, Fire Rescue Magazine, (November 21, 2016). Retrieved from https://www.firerescuemagazine.com/articles/2016/11/mgm-grand-hotel-fire-anniversary.html

[22] MGM Fire Investigation, Fire Scene Examination, Initial Response, Clark County Fire Department, VIII-2. Available at https://www.firerescuemagazine.com/content/dam/fe/downloads/FFN-FRM-Downloads-Editorial/MGM_FIRE.pdf

[23] *Id.*

hotel through the elevator shafts, the air handling system and then the stairwells and seismic joints. Fire alarms were sounding in the hotel. Guests emerged from their rooms and ran for the exits; luckily, thousands escaped. Over time, the smoke became so heavy and acrid that the ability of the awakened guests to use exits and evacuate the hotel diminished. Soon thereafter that option ended. The smoke overcame some guests, who died in the stairwells. Other guests who did not respond to the alarms died in their hotel rooms. Meanwhile, large helicopters were flown in from a nearby air force base and evacuated more than 1,000 guests from the roof of the hotel.

At the end of this tragic day, 85 people were dead, and more than 600 people were injured by the toxic smoke.[24] The event had wide, graphic news and TV coverage and shocked not just Las Vegas but the entire country.

Unlike the Supper Club fire that occurred three years earlier, the MGM Grand was a large and successful enterprise and relatively wealthy. It possessed not only a $25 million insurance policy but also significant assets to respond to the victims claims for damages. The MGM corporation was listed on the New York Stock Exchange. The fire disaster and potential for claims caused its stock to tumble.

The MGM Grand Fire Litigation quickly surpassed the Supper Club Litigation as the largest Mass Tort in U.S. history. Plaintiff's attorneys descended on Las Vegas in droves seeking fire victims to represent. After all, it was Las Vegas. What better venue to spend leisure time and obtain big attorney's fees with contingency fee cases? Well known plaintiff's lawyers came from Louisiana, Texas, Florida, Illinois, Ohio,

---

[24] MGM Grand Hotel Fire Anniversary, Read the reports on what led up to this deadly fire and how firefighter's responder, Fire Rescue Magazine, (November 21, 2016). Retrieved from https://www.firerescuemagazine.com/articles/2016/11/mgm-grand-hotel-fire-anniversary.html

California and, of course, Las Vegas.

Then the lawsuits began, many of them. The lawyers also began to posture themselves to become "lead" lawyers, so that they would have the biggest roles and receive the biggest fees. In due time, all the lawsuits were consolidated into the United States District Court in Las Vegas. It became the "MGM Grand Fire Litigation." Judge Louis Bechtel, a United States District Court Judge in Philadelphia, was assigned to manage the case.

I believe as many as 1,327 lawsuits were filed against 118 companies. One thing was obvious. The MGM Grand Hotel was not occupied by only ordinary folks. It was a grand and expensive venue attracting both gamblers and vacationers, which included some high rollers. Many of the injured victims and the decedent's estates would have large damage claims. Amalgamating them together would produce claims for potentially hundreds of millions of dollars in damages, huge claims in 1980. Thus, the larger the litigation and the more defendants you bring into it, the more insurance monies you may be able to tap into for settlements. The cost of defense of such massive litigation can produce handsome settlement pots with the motto, "the more defendants, the better." In essence, the MGM Grand Fire Litigation portended a true feeding frenzy for lawyers, both for the plaintiffs and for the defendants.

The first and most obvious case was the potential liability of the MGM Grand for the hotel fire. It purchased more insurance, so it now had a $50 million insurance nest egg. In round numbers, that could amass $16.5 million in attorneys' fees at a thirty-three percent contingency fee. But the MGM Grand was not a boat "dead in the water." It had defenses to the claims that could not be asserted by the Supper Club in its fire.

The hotel had complied with the applicable fire codes. The Deli and the casino were not required to be sprinklered. The sprinklers operated and prevented the fire from spreading to the upper floors. The fire triggered the fire alarms, sounding a warning to evacuate. Over 4,000 guests escaped successfully. The hotel staff held fire training practices for its employees. No employee of the hotel acted improperly during the fire. The Deli was empty, as was the casino but for seven people. There was no prior history of casino fires to demonstrate the risk of such a large and fast-moving fire within a casino environment.

That said, the MGM Grand was still facing a gauntlet of potential claims in the massive litigation. It had minor fire code issues and construction mistakes that aided the spread of smoke to the upper floors. If the Deli was no longer open for 24 hours, sprinklers should have been installed. There were other issues as well.

At the end of the day, you cannot find more innocent victims than the hotel guests asleep in their rooms. Someone was going to pay for this one way or another. Many of them could be targeted companies that supplied furniture and materials that burned in the fire ala the earlier Supper Club lawsuits.

When the MGM Grand Litigation expanded to sue the manufacturers of the furnishings and other products that burned in the fire, they sued a number of electrical wire companies. They also sued two PVC producers, BF Goodrich Company and Conoco, Inc., both of whom retained my law firm to defend them.

When I arrived in Las Vegas, the MGM Grand Hotel Fire Litigation was over a year old. My two clients were sued in the Master Complaint filed just prior to the expiration of the one-year statute of limitations which would have barred the lawsuits. We were part of the dozens of new defendants alleged to have supplied "dangerous" products and materials that had burned in the casino fire. It was shades of the Supper Club Fire Litigation.

Judge Louis Bechtel was running the case. He was an excellent choice: smart, tough, experienced and moving the case apace. He divided the case into four divisions. The first addressed the liability of the MGM Grand and its related entities. The second addressed a group of companies and professionals that participated in the construction and recent remodeling of the hotel. The third involved the lawsuits against and among dozens of insurance companies who had sold insurance policies for some part of the entire insurance regime. The fourth was our group of product producers to defend the product liability claims.

The U.S. District Court house in Las Vegas was large. When I attended our first Pre-Trial Conference, sitting at the table for the plaintiffs were: the Plaintiff's Legal Committee ("PLC"): John J. Cumming, III, New Orleans, La., Stanley M. Chesley, Cincinnati, Ohio, Wendell H. Gauthier, Kenner, La., Melvin M. Belli, San Francisco, Cal., Toxey H. Smith, Los Angeles, Cal., Will S. Kemp, Las Vegas, Nev., Joseph W. Cotchell, San Mateo, Cal., Leonard M. Ring, Chicago, Ill., J. Bruce Alverson, Las Vegas, Nev., Joseph Weiner, Philadelphia, Pa. It was a foreboding array of the best-known plaintiff's lawyers in the country. This MGM Grand Hotel Fire Litigation was going to be big, indeed.

In managing the litigation, Judge Bechtel relied heavily on the Plaintiff's Lead Counsel ("PLC") he named from among those attorneys. He summed up the work of his appointed PLC in his second published judicial opinion:

> "Many of the attorneys who ultimately became PLC members of the 12-member committee conducted an extensive on-site investigation at the MGM Grand Hotel in Las Vegas and hired, at their expense, experts to study the site before the demolition and rebuilding of the affected areas of the hotel. The PLC recovered over 6,000 objects from the fire site and stored and used them in a joint warehouse depository during the course of this litigation. It hired some of the best experts in the nation to test various products found in the hotel at substantial expense and retained an 'in

house' expert to coordinate all experts and supervise a substantial regimen of testing. The PLC established a document depository, reviewed (which included cataloguing and some microfilming) over 4,000,000 documents produced by the various defendants, and organized and catalogued all information gleaned by computer for retrieval by subject categories.

"The PLC members participated in and supervised the taking of over 1,400 depositions, in "tracks" of up to 11 depositions in different cities at one time, and prepared summaries of all relevant depositions for the trial of the case. It reviewed every deposition transcript and designated each section expected to be used at trial. The PLC completed all aspects of all waves of discovery in accordance with the *Manual for Complex Litigation.*

"The PLC filed pleadings on behalf of all plaintiffs, including original and amended complaints and all discovery pleadings in state and federal courts across the country and in the United States Court of Appeals for the Ninth Circuit. It was eventually successful in having all claims filed in this court thereby permitting claims which had originally been filed in many federal district and state courts to proceed together. The PLC reviewed and responded to thousands of items of correspondence and pleadings by the defendants and initiated substantial correspondence and hundreds of pleadings on behalf of all the 1,000 or so plaintiffs. It prepared and filed extensive motions, applications, and briefs relative to Nevada's "Statute of Repose"; "choice of law'" bifurcation; punitive damages; discovery; disqualifications; severance, and all of the other relevant aspects of this litigation. As noted above, the PLC prepared the single amended complaint for all plaintiffs' interests. It prepared agendas for and attended all pre-trial conferences with this court

> including weekly and bi-weekly discovery and dispute hearings before the Magistrate, and prepared pleadings for and appeared at more than 225 pretrial hearings over the course of the litigation, including the handling of in excess of 1,000 motions dealing with discovery issues. The PLC coordinated the compilation of damage material in each individual case, participating in the preparation of answers and/or objections to all damage interrogatories.
>
> "The PLC was successful in having trial dates set in succession against various groups of defendants in order to conduct the trial in the most expeditious manner. It marshalled over 11,000 relevant documents for trial, prepared dozens of witnesses for trial, prepared an extensive pretrial order and jury trial books. It conducted a demographic jury poll to analyze the likelihood of success in the Nevada courts against selected defendants." *See; In Re MGM Grand Hotel Fire Litigation*, 660 F. Supp. 522, 523-24 (D. Nev 1987).

My part of the case was designed by Stan Chesley from Cincinnati. It followed the same template as in the Supper Club to sue PVC. The PLC retained Terry Hoyle to present their case. He was formerly a fire chief in Chicago. When he retired, he started a fire safety consulting business. The MGM Grand fire would launch his career. He took charge of the fire scene investigation, detailing the alleged products and materials that had burned and the alleged contribution of each product to the fire and toxicity of the smoke. He then studied each product and material to identify its fire performance and toxic by-products when burning. His report filled twelve hundred pages and eight loose leaf binders. We all read it looking for the pages reporting on our client's product. The allegations against PVC were not new. At Terry Hoyle's lengthy deposition, I held him to his opinion in his report, so

I believed we could defend our clients successfully in a fair trial.

At our first Products Group Pre-Trial Conference, about twenty-eight defense lawyers attended representing the various defendants. Judge Bechtel issued a Scheduling Order for discovery in the products case. The lawyer representing the wire companies was David Sprowl from San Diego. When we met, we both came to the same conclusion. We needed each other! David was young, but wise beyond his years and fearless. This litigation did not intimidate him. I had a PVC defense in hand, tested in three trials. We were confident we could defend the wire and its insulation.

Judge Bechtel devised a case management strategy for the case and that strategy proved most effective. First, there was a Scheduling Order that accelerated and combined discovery. Often up to a dozen depositions were occurring daily. When the Scheduling Order time period closed, in theory it was time for the trial. But how soon? Normally, months intervened for trial organization and preparation but not in Las Vegas. Judge Bechtel intended to start the trial quickly — in two weeks in one instance. This panicked the defense attorneys. They were then handed off to the court-appointed Settlement Coordinator who facilitated and mediated settlements. The settlements were fast and large. The MGM Grand Hotel Fire Litigation was being "managed" expertly by Judge Bechtel. The settlements were piling up millions of dollars in cash. I do not recall that any case ever went through the threatened jury trial.

When our products discovery closed, we attended our final Pre-Trial conference. Judge Bechtel proposed a very quick trial date and many of the defense lawyers protested. This was a large and, in many respects to most of them, a new and unique case. They argued that time was required to prepare for trial. David and I sat there saying nothing. Our trial defense was already in place. We could go to trial in two weeks, if necessary. The products case was moved to the Settlement

Coordinator. The defense costs were high — pay your money, fold your tent and go home.

To conduct settlement negotiations, we were assigned to PLC member Wendell Gauthier from Metairie, Louisiana. Wendell was a seasoned and rich lawyer. He had won many cases for plaintiffs with big verdicts in New Orleans. He was one of the owners of the large casino in downtown New Orleans. Prior to being a lawyer, he had been a boxer. He was short, strong, experienced and tough with a crocodile smile. He lived in a mansion on a ranch near New Orleans. We would negotiate our settlement with Wendell at his home.

When I flew to New Orleans for the conference, I collected my carry-on bag and headed to the door for a taxi. I spotted a person holding a sign that said "Henlein." Wendell sent a car for me. The person holding the sign resembled a Dallas Cowboy cheerleader. She was blonde, wearing a white blouse, white vest, white mini skirt and white boots. She took me outside to a parked white Rolls Royce with a large Cajun driver. We rode to the ranch together in the back seat.

At the ranch David was waiting for me. We agreed on two things for sure: this would be interesting, and we would curtail our drinking at cocktail hour. We had a splendid dinner with Wendell.

The next morning, we met to negotiate a settlement for our clients. Wendell described the problems of winning a trial in a place like Las Vegas where the fire was big news. He had previously negotiated the settlement of a carpet padding supplier, General Felt Products of California, Inc., for $175,000. He said the wire was present at the beginning of the alleged electrical fire and PVC was present on it and throughout the casino in chair and table covers, and more. Therefore, our clients each owed more than that amount. He was thinking at least $300,000 from each of our defendants. He wanted our response. I advised him of my prior trial experience and success for PVC in wire fires; we were ready to go to trial on short notice. We were confident we could win for PVC and wire again. His product liability case against us was a loser. Even Terry Hoyle, the fire investigation specialist, could not save it. I had pinned him down in his earlier deposition. Wendell was amazed!

David described how, if we forced a jury trial, Judge Bechtel's speeding settlement machine would have to shut down to accommodate our trial. Moreover, if we win, other defendants might see their way forward to do the same thing. The settlement train could be derailed. The meeting adjourned for over an hour. We presumed Wendell was calling other PLC members to report our heresy. By noon, we had reached an agreement. Each defendant would pay a reasonable defense cost of $50,000. We left Louisiana with satisfied clients and then I left Las Vegas; I was richer and wiser for the experience.

Meanwhile, with our case settled in Louisiana, the other products and material defendants were also settling. In fact, every defendant in the entire MGM Grand case settled. Judge Bechtel approved every settlement. In his 1987 Memorandum and Order[25], he cited the Coopers & Lybrand Audit Report of total settlement receipts of $203,393,228. He had evaluated the claims at $350 million, as he reported in his Order. He had accomplished a remarkable disposition of so many claims and such a large litigation with over $200,000,000 recovered.

What followed was Judge Bechtel wrangling with all the PLC members and individual lawyers representing each plaintiff over their attorney fees. Without going into all the details — which were many — it appears the attorney's fees he awarded, in gross, were around thirty-three percent (33%); this would be $66,000,000. It was good to be a plaintiff's lawyer in Las Vegas.

Later, an insurance company auditor attempted to assess the damage, *i.e.* what was the total cost to the industry to

[25] In Re MGM Grand Hotel Fire Litigation, 570 F. Supp. 913 (D. Nev. 1983).

defend all the MGM Grand litigation. In essence, this was attorney's fees for hundreds of lawyers. He produced an estimate of $250 million. If accurate, the total cost to the insurance industry of the MGM Grand fire and the resulting litigation, including all settlements, was over $450 million dollars. The claimants received only 40 percent; lawyers got most of the rest.

The complexities of the MGM Grand Hotel Fire Litigation speak volumes. No litigation resembling it would ever occur in England, or elsewhere. It was unique to the United States. If an identical fire would have occurred in a similar hotel in England, the litigation would not be the same. Although there would be similarities in the legal principles of Tort, product liability and insurance, any lawsuits that resulted would be categorically different.

Perhaps most important, had the MGM Grand case been brought in England with the English Rule, most of the product defendants would not have been sued at all. If they had been sued and asserted valid defenses — which most of them had — the English Rule would have been enforced. The defendants and their insurers would have recovered their large attorney's fees. There is a price to pay for suing an innocent defendant in England — but not in the U.S.

The threat of a trial before a citizen jury, as in Las Vegas, does not exist in England. Any trial would be before an unemotional, experienced Senior Judge. Judge Bechtel was an excellent judge for the MGM Grand Hotel Fire Litigation. He got the job done. He was a judge with the qualifications to be a Judge in London, high praise, indeed. But his role in London would not be the same as in America.

By having a contingency fee of 33 percent as a golden carrot, the PLC was incentivized to make the case and its settlement train as large, long and cumbersome as possible. The bigger the litigation train, the bigger the cost of defense settlements. The more work a PLC lawyer did, the bigger the contingency fee he would receive. In England, they would be working for their regular hourly rates; the rate of pay would be the same for a big case or a small one. They would not own any part of the plaintiffs' claims.

The comparison of the English and American civil legal systems can best be made by looking at a similar fire in London. On June 15, 2017, a fire broke out at the Glenfell Tower in Notting Hill. It began on the eighth floor and burned up the interior and exterior of the 23-story building. The Tower was built forty years earlier. It did not have sprinklers and had flammable cladding panels on the exterior. Seventy-nine people were killed — six less than in the MGM Grand fire — and dozens were hospitalized.

Searching online, 15 months later, I found only one lawsuit. It is a shareholder class action filed in New York City against Arconic, the cladding company. Remember, fifteen months after the MGM Grand fire, the Master Complaint had been filed and the litigation was running amok. Only in America was the MGM Grand litigation possible.

AIR CANADA FLIGHT 797 (1983)

When we fly on an airplane, we accept that we are in control of nothing. We relax and trust the pilots and crew. From time to time, we learn about a plane crash where the passengers and crew died. Each plane crash is a Mass Tort tragedy. In this next case, some passengers survived but many did not.

On the morning of June 2, 1983, it was a sky-blue day in Dallas, Texas. The McDonnell Douglas DC9 Air Canada Flight 797 taxied down the runway and took off. It was flying from the Dallas/Fort Worth International Airport bound for Montreal, Canada. On board were two pilots, three crew members and 41 passengers. Among the passengers were Stan Rogers, a famous Canadian singer, Curtis Mathis, the scion of a Texas family-owned TV and appliance manufacturing business and five senior executives of a large Canadian corporation. There was also a group of Canadian tourists scattered in the seats among other U.S. passengers. Many rows were empty. Unbeknownst to all on board, a fire of mysterious origin started beneath the bathroom floor in the rear of the plane. No one was sitting that far back, so the fire went undetected. It silently penetrated the bathroom. Smoke began to seep into the passenger compartment. The smoke was noticed by the crew.

The plane was now entering Missouri air space. It could have diverted its course to make an emergency landing at St. Louis Lambert International Airport. It did not. Instead, the co-pilot and crew investigated. They believed the fire was contained in the bathroom trash can although the smoke obscured their vision. They reported this belief to the Captain. The decision was made to attempt to extinguish the trash can fire. It was the wrong decision. The fire continued to grow.

The plane was now entering Kentucky air space. It could have diverted to an emergency landing at Standiford Field in Louisville. It did not. Billowing smoke was now filling the plane. The passengers were moved to the front of the plane and given wet hand towels to cover their faces.

Finally, the decision was made to divert the course and land at the Greater Cincinnati International Airport located in northern Kentucky. Meanwhile, the smoke in the plane was hanging heavy and acrid in the cabin. The fire burned through the bathroom wall. It entered the plane cabin searching for new fuel. The plane's flammable seats were readily available, but the fire was growing slowly at this stage.

All fires require three things: heat, fuel and a source of oxygen. Without any one of these sources the fire will die. To cut off fuel, an often-used tactic to fight forest fires is to set another fire in the path of the advancing fire. This is called backfiring. This secondary fire burns up the fuel the forest fire would require to continue its burning advance. Without new fuel, the forest fire dies. On the other hand, if you can cut off air, a small fire is easily extinguished by smothering it with a blanket or dousing it with water.

The fire on 797 was growing slowly because the supply of air in the plane was limited by the sealed metal fuselage. In fact, the fire and the passengers were now locked into a competition to consume the air in the plane. The oxygen masks could not be dropped and turned on. That would have given fresh air to the nascent fire.

The plane landed safely at the airport and taxied to an adjacent runway. The pilot was lauded for managing to land so well under such difficult circumstances. Waiting on the runway was an array of fire trucks, firefighting equipment and firefighters.

The cabin door was opened. A life and death race ensued. Passengers surged forward and began tumbling out of the plane. The fire also detected the fresh air supply at the open door. It came forward to consume the fresh air. It filled the plane with intense heat and smoke as seats were set ablaze. Tragically, the fire beat twenty-three passengers to the open door.[26] They died in the plane, some from asphyxiation and others from the intense heat.

The smoke and flames poured out the open door and into the sky. The plane fire continued to burn for hours. The plume of smoke was easily visible in the city of Cincinnati across the Ohio river from the airport in northern Kentucky. It was even seen as far as 89 miles away in Lexington, Kentucky. Among the dead was the appliance scion, the five executives and the singer.

There was a legal complication present in this tragic plane disaster. Because the flight was between the United States airport in Dallas and the Canadian airport in Montreal, it was designated as an "international" flight. The United States and 136 other countries had signed a treaty covering international plane disasters. The Warsaw Convention limited damages recoverable by a deceased passenger from any airline on an international flight to $75,000.[27] Thus, even if the disaster was caused by the Captain of the Air Canada flight for not diverting and landing in St. Louis, the maximum total monies available to the estates of the victims from the airline would be $1.725 million (23 X $75,000). That amount was less than the scion had earned in 1982, the year before his death. The damage claim for his death by his estate, under U.S. law,

---

[26] Airlive, #OnThisDay ini 1983, Air Canada Flight 797 developed an in-flight fire behind thee lavatory (June 2, 2018) available at http://www.airlive.net/onthisday-in-1983-air-canada-flight-797-developed-an-in-flight-fire-behind-the-lavatory/

[27] Convention for the unification of certain rules related to international carriage by air, signed at Warsaw on 12 October 1929 (Warsaw Convention), Chapter III Articles 17-22 (amended in 1955 and 1975). Available at https://www.jus.uio.no/lm/air.carriage.warsaw.convention.1929/doc.html#91

would have been twenty-three times that total amount, which is his life expectancy multiplied by his earnings. Instead, his estate received only $75,000 dollars, as did the other estates, paid by the Air Canada airline.

Because the flight was international, the lawyers who arrived began searching for someone to sue. The McDonnell Douglas DC9 was an obvious target but the plane was built in accordance with FAA standards. Who else could the lawyers dream up? Lawyers can be creative when seeking new lawsuits.

Lawsuits were filed against McDonnell Douglas for building a plane that caught on fire. This was a classic product liability claim. They were looking for something about that plane to be defective! The first suits were filed in St. Louis where McDonnell Douglas is located and northern Kentucky, where the plane landed, and the deaths and injuries occurred. Other suits were later filed in Houston, where several passengers lived. As expected, all the suits were consolidated into a single United States District Court, as occurred in the MGM Grand Litigation. This was the United States District Court for the Central District of California in Los Angeles where Judge Laughlin Edwin Waters, Sr. resided. He turned out to be a fair and excellent choice.

After filing suits against McDonnell Douglas, the plaintiffs sought discovery to find the manufacturers of the products on the plane that had burned in the fire. This included the seats, the foam in the seats and their cloth covers. Their manufacturers were sued. The carpet company and the plastic company that supplied the material for the bathroom walls, door and floor were revealed. They were sued as well. There were not many defendants to name, unlike the Supper Club and MGM Grand.

The polyurethane foam company they sued was Tenneco, Inc. I was retained to represent them. I had successful experience defending polyurethane foam in other smaller fire lawsuits. I had previously-retained experts to rely on. I had used the Tenneco Research and Development Vice President, Wayne Sorenson, as a witness in the Supper Club case where Tenneco was a defendant.

At the first Pre-Trial Conference in Los Angeles, lawyers for the defendants appeared. Judge Waters certified the case as a class action. He was correct. All the plaintiff's claims were identical, based on the same facts in the plane. He then invited the attorneys to submit a pre-trial scheduling order, appointing attorneys from both sides to do so. I was not one of them. I was fine with that. I wanted an unnoticed role for an innocent product supplier. We met after the conference and formed a "plane seat defense group" to consolidate our defense for the case. We were a defense team of four. It was a straightforward defense.

McDonnell Douglas was a "sophisticated purchaser" of plane materials. That means it did not rely on its material suppliers to tell them which seat foam or cover to use on the seats. It was building its plane to Federal Aviation Authority ("FAA") specifications for planes along with its own corporate specifications for its planes. As a rule, this is an ironclad defense for a foam supplier, so long as its foam meets the purchaser's demanded specifications. McDonnell Douglas conducted quality control tests of the materials it purchased and used. The tests of Tenneco's foam for the seats in this plane passed the tests.

Once we proved these facts, we were in a position to file a Federal Rule of Civil Procedure 56 Motion for Summary Judgement, as we had done in the Yonkers litigation after the trial. These facts were beyond dispute, the case law was clear, and we were entitled to be dismissed as a matter of law. All the plaintiffs could argue was that Tenneco could have supplied foam that was flame retardant and therefore, should have done so.

Tenneco did manufacture flame retardant foam for special end uses specified by the buyer. For instance, flame-retardant foam is mandated for acoustic foam used to dampen sound in public buildings. Fire codes mandate it. In some states, flame retardant foam is mandated in baby crib mattresses. There are other examples, but the plaintiff's averred claim in this case was an empty bucket. The FAA and McDonnell Douglas did not mandate flame-retardant foam for two reasons. First, adding the flame-retarding chemical diminishes the cushioning and longevity of the foam significantly. Therefore, it is not used in seats. Airplane seats receive a lot of use by people of every weight. The life of flame-retardant foam in plane seats would be much lower than the specified, higher density cushioning foam for planes. Second, adding flame retardants make the foam more dense and heavier. Weight is a paramount consideration for an airplane. Our defenses defeated their averment.

We prepared and filed our Motion for Summary Judgement and supporting legal Memorandum. Judge Waters granted it without requiring an oral argument, dismissing the case. The law worked as it should. I left the case and do not know the ending for the other defendants.

This case is a perfect illustration of how contingency fees make lawyers in America into ambulance chasers. The dismissal does not change the conclusion that if this plane were made in England and landed on fire in London, lawsuits against the seats and their components would never have been filed. If they had been filed, we would have recovered our attorney's fees. That said, however, with Judge Waters, justice was served.

SAN JUAN DUPONT PLAZA HOTEL (1988)

What is the cumulative effect of too many lawyers, contingency fees, political judges, the American Rule and jury trials for civil cases? One of my biggest Mass Tort cases presents a perfect case study.

Puerto Rico is a large island in the Caribbean. It has an interesting history with the United States. In 1889, it became a United States territory. Both Alaska and Hawaii were also U.S. Territories. They became states in 1959. Despite Puerto Rico's petition to become a state in the past, it never became one. It was not either strategically as important as Hawaii or as resource rich as Alaska, and its native language is Spanish. It could not overcome these issues.

San Juan is the capital. On the eastern shore of San Juan is a tall rocky bluff. Atop the bluff is the Fortaleza, complete with old cannon turrets to repel pirates in an earlier time. The Fortaleza, a castle, is the home to the Governor of Puerto Rico. Historically he was appointed by the President of the United States for a four-year term. He is elected today. The Governor overees the Puerto Rico legislature, which governs the country. Because Puerto Rico is a territory, it has a United States District Court as does Guam, another territory, and every state in the United States.

Puerto Rican citizens became American citizens in 1917. At that time, the Governor was Arthur Yager who served for eight years. He had the good fortune to attend both Princeton and Johns Hopkins universities with Woodrow Wilson. He was the President of Georgetown College when he was called to accept his appointment as Governor of Puerto Rico. He moved his family to the Fortaleza in 1913. My mother was his daughter, she was thirteen-years old at the time; he was my grandfather. Throughout my mother's life, I heard stories about her time in Puerto Rico.

The island was a paradise for sun-seeking vacationers to the Caribbean in the 1980s. On Seven Mile Beach, rated one of the most beautiful beaches in the world, are several high-rise condominiums, similar to Miami Beach and Ft. Lauderdale. There were three high-rise casino hotels, like those in Las Vegas, but with white sand beaches and scenic views of the blue-green ocean. The hotels included the Condado Plaza Hotel, the San Juan Dupont Plaza Hotel and the Hyatt Beach Hotel and Casino. All were very plush, indeed.

On December 31, 1986, it was a sunny day in Puerto Rico. The San Juan Dupont Plaza had 22 floors, 450 rooms, and was directly on the Seven Mile Beach. It was New Year's Eve, so the hotel was full of guests. On the ground floor was a large ballroom that opened into a broad stairway leading into a second-floor lobby where the large casino was located. The casino resembled those in other gaming hotels. There was a bank of slot machines just inside the lobby doors, gambling tables, furniture and a bar. It was a typical gaudy casino and popular. It did not have windows overlooking the beach and pool behind the hotel that could lure gamblers away from the gaming tables. The few windows it did have overlooked the parking lot in the front. That morning about 100 guests were already in the casino. Many others were at the beach or the pool.

That same morning, the Teamsters Union was having a meeting downstairs in the ballroom. A labor dispute with the hotel was boiling over and the Teamsters represented more than half of the hotel's employees. The Teamsters were having a vote to strike, so trouble was on the horizon. No one knew how much trouble that would be.

In Puerto Rico, labor disputes often turn nasty. After a strike vote, it was typical for mysterious fires to occur at the disputed business. In fact, three small fires had been set in the

Dupont Plaza hotel closets the week before. On this day, three Teamsters decided a small fire was needed to focus the hotel on their demands. Around 3:30 p.m., they set out to do just that.

The ballroom where the Teamsters were meeting had three large accordion doors that could be closed to divide the ballroom into three rooms. The door toward the back of the ballroom was closed. Large cardboard boxes of new furniture were stored behind it. Two of the upper floors were being remodeled and the new furniture was for those remodeled rooms. The stored boxes contained sofa beds, carpets, beds, mattresses, chairs, tables, and so on. Three Teamsters took small cans of Sterno into the storage area. They lit them and placed them against two large boxes. This small fire, they believed, would get the negotiations on track. Then all 150 Teamsters left the building and drove away.

The hotel was not actively sprinklered. No hotel employee was present in the ballroom. The Sterno cans set two of the large cardboard boxes containing Sealy sofa beds on fire. The sofa beds were of common design, made of wood with polyurethane foam mattresses and cushions covered with nylon cloth. Fire safety engineers describe polyurethane foam, made with petrochemicals, as "solid gasoline." Once on fire, the foam can burn rapidly. The cardboard flamed up, burned through, and set fire to the mattresses and cushions inside. That was all that was needed to set ablaze all the boxes, with their foam, plastic and wood contents. The other furniture also caught on fire. Soon the curtain divider was ablaze. Then it disappeared. A fire was engulfing the ballroom and coming up the grand stairway to the lobby... and the casino. The super-heated smoke and gases roared into the lobby and then into the casino through the open double doors. The gamblers were now trapped. Hotel management had locked the emergency exits to avoid thefts. The only exit was the double doors that were already owned by the fire. Most of the guests died there... 86 patrons. The bodies were charred beyond recognition. Only a few managed to break the windows and jump to the concrete ground below. As was learned in the MGM Grand fire, casinos are flammable.

The elevators were called to the lobby by the call inset buttons that respond to the heat of your hand to activate. These hand pads were commonly used by Otis-designed elevators at that time. The fire heated the pads and the elevators came to the lobby where their doors opened and the fire greeted the passengers. Twelve passengers were burned alive instantly.

As was the case in the MGM Grand fire, some hotel guests migrated upward to the roof. There, approximately 600 were rescued by helicopters. It was all recorded by San Juan TV stations. It was horrible. The fire disaster devastated San Juan and Puerto Rico. Most of the 98 deaths were in the casino and elevators. Many others were injured by smoke inhalation.

Some of the hotel guests forced to jump from the second-floor casino windows suffered orthopedic injuries with two confined to wheelchairs for the rest of their lives. The total serious injuries were 140. The 960 guests who escaped were traumatized and many of them had smoke inhalation claims.

There was no alarm or warning of the fire or its rapid spread. That said, a security guard passing by the full-length ballroom windows noticed the smoke. He had not been trained in fire safety. He did not know what to do, so he went looking for his supervisor. He located him about eight minutes later. When they returned to the ballroom to look in the windows, all they saw were walls of flame.

The TV coverage brought people to the scene. They saw the tragedy unfold first-hand. This included keen interest in the many helicopter landings on the roof removing hotel guests. One of those observing the fire scene was Raymond Acosta, who would play an important role in the future litigation of this tragedy.

The three Teamster arsonists were quickly arrested, then convicted. They were each sentenced to 99 years in prison and were placed in isolation for fear of retaliation from Puerto Rican inmates.

The lawyers began to arrive in search of their contingency fees. Two of the plaintiff's lawyers were in the MGM Grand litigation, Stanley Chesley and Wendell Gauthier. They knew what to do. It would be *déjà vu,* all over again. They were joined by an array of San Juan lawyers. They formed a 12-member Plaintiffs Legal Committee ("PLC"). They were accomplished and successful lawyers. Lawsuits were filed, ultimately 264 of them for 1,200 plaintiffs (including one dog) seeking $1.8 billion dollars from 230 defendants. The Dupont Plaza Hotel Fire Litigation would rival the MGM Grand Litigation to be one of the largest Mass Tort litigations in United States history.

However, the DuPont Plaza Fire Litigation defense would not be the same as the other Mass Tort fire lawsuits preceding it. The Supper Club and MGM Grand fire litigations presented the worst that America could possibly offer. They were not part of a "just, fair, and inexpensive legal system."

It dawned on me that we had to fight fire with fire to overcome these huge contingency fee driven Mass Tort lawsuits. The critical decision was not if the judge was inexperienced as in the Super Club or experienced as in the MGM Grand. The result was the same for both. The critical decision would be how the companies and their insurers responded to being sued in another similar Mass Tort. Rather than each defendant hiring a lawyer (really lawyers — plural — in suits this big) why not combine all the defendants together with fewer lawyers? This would reduce the "cost of defense" settlement demands everyone had to pay because of the huge lawyer fees. Under my scenario, the more defendants that are sued the better; the cost of defense expense for each defendant would now be less when the cost is shared. The math will work for the defendants rather than against them.

Second, if the defendants had gone to trial in the MGM Grand Litigation, the whole coerced settlement strategy would have imploded. So now that we could control defense costs, why not go forward and win the trial? After all, the defendants are innocent. In San Juan, they did not cause the fire or the resulting disaster. The Teamsters and the hotel's mistakes, obviously injured and killed the hotel guests. They should bear the entire liability.

I decided to see if these two strategies could be employed successfully. How could it be worse than the MGM Grand Litigation where the insurers spent $250 million dollars in defense costs to produce $200 million dollars in paid settlements? Further, logic told me that if this new defense strategy were successful, it could foretell the end of these catastrophic fire mass tort lawsuits in the future.

Shortly after the fire, I suggested a joint defense strategy to the attorneys at Dupont, BFGoodrich and Occidental Petroleum. A conference was scheduled in Wilmington, Delaware to review my plan. We met and decided on a dual defense strategy. First, all the petrochemical companies would band together to jointly defend the lawsuits with one law firm. Further, the case should not be settled but be taken through trial. It was an arson fire so it could be won. This dual strategy would overcome the big cost of defense settlements. We could end this vicious cycle in these large fire disasters.

I returned to Louisville with three clients, expecting more to come. One of my favorite expressions is "beware the law of unintended consequences." Another is "be careful what you wish for, it may come true." Little did I know what I had wished for. I spent thirteen months as the court appointed Lead Defense Counsel in a trial in a San Juan federal court in one of the largest lawsuits ever.

All the lawsuits became consolidated in the United States District Court for Puerto Rico in San Juan. It was an English-speaking court in a Spanish speaking territory. It was assigned to U.S. District Court Judge Raymond L. Acosta. He had been appointed in 1982, four years prior. I understood he was appointed because his sister was married to the Governor, politics again. Before being appointed, he was a trusts and estates lawyer. He was without any experience to manage such a case. Moreover, he would not have been a judge at all in England, much less assigned to a case as important as this.

The next strategy was to appear in court and defend the massive Master Complaint before it was filed. The plaintiff's strategy was to file a quick lawsuit to gain control of the fire scene. Under court supervision, their experts would then be allowed early entry to the fire scene to find cause and origin evidence. They would also be looking for anyone and everyone they could identify to sue. That is exactly what Terry Hoyle, the fire expert witness, had done in the MGM Grand fire litigation. After all that could be completed, and before the one-year statute of limitations could run out, they would draft and file the Master Complaint against all the new defendants. By the time the defense fire experts could arrive, the fire scene would be stale — or gone. In the Supper Club fire, the building had been razed.

This put the defense at a distinct disadvantage. The defense experts would not get to see the supporting evidence the plaintiffs' experts alleged they saw. When questioned closely on any far-out opinion, the plaintiffs' experts could say, "I saw it at the scene." The defense experts would have to rely on the investigative work of others. I wanted equal footing for our defense.

As predicted, at the first pre-trial conference in San Juan, the plaintiff's lawyers sought control of the hotel fire scene after the arson crime investigation was closed. We also appeared in court. The U.S. Magistrate Judge Justo Arenas conducted the hearing. He, and everyone else present, was surprised when our appearance was entered. The plaintiff's lawyers clamored that we could not appear in court, we had no sued party to defend. They demanded to know who our clients were. Technically, they were correct; we had no standing. Since we had no standing, we did not have to reveal our clients. We advised the court that if the plaintiffs' counsel would represent to the court that they had no intention of filing a future Master Complaint naming more than 100 new defendants, we would be more than happy to leave the courtroom. Outrage was building across the room, but no representation was offered. Judge Arenas — who turned out to be excellent and impartial in this instance — sat looking thoughtfully. We offered a second option. If we were denied equal access to the arson scene, then at trial if any fire expert offered an opinion based on his fire scene investigation, it could be stricken. Surely our adversaries would agree to that fair resolution. Again, silence from the other side. Ten days after the hearing, lawyers from my firm, with our selected fire experts, entered the fire scene with the plaintiff's lawyers and their experts.

The San Juan Dupont Plaza Hotel Fire Litigation was divided into three phases. Although under-insured, the hotel did have insurance coverage. The hotel's insurance coverage was the first target. After much skirmishing, the insurers settled by paying $50 million.

Next came the hotel owners, whoever they were. The liability of the hotel was so obvious, the owners' assets would be pursued. The ownership passed through an array and labyrinth of corporations and partnerships, many located in Texas and California. Unraveling and piercing it all was a large task, which in the end led to a three-month jury trial for many of them. Ultimately, it appeared that three wealthy Californians were the owners. At the end of the day, $35 million was recovered. Peripheral insurers offered another $15 million in soft money; money they hoped to find and raise in the future. There was now $100 million in the settlement pot.

Last came the claims against the furniture and products involved in the fire in the hotel. A year after the fire, the Master Complaint was filed against some 100 companies that supplied products or materials to the hotel, either directly or indirectly, exactly what happened with the MGM Grand.

The Master Complaint looked something like this: Sealy

Sofa Company was sued for the sofa beds which burned in the initial fire. The component suppliers of the sofa beds were then revealed by Sealy in discovery. Those named suppliers were also sued because the material they supplied burned when the sofa burned. For instance, Georgia Pacific Corporation was sued for the cardboard box material and Weyerhaeuser Corporation was sued for the wood crate. Dupont was sued for the nylon cushion covers. Foamex/Scott Foam Corp was sued for the foam cushions and mattresses. The chemical companies, BASF, Dow Chemical, Occidental Petroleum and Quantum Chemical were sued for the raw chemicals used to make the foam. Each of the six sofa beds produced claims against ten defendants. The plaintiffs' attorneys envisioned the MGM Grand "costs of defense" scheme magnifying along with their contingency fees.

They followed the same approach for carpets, drapes, furniture, gaming tables, etc. Sue the product, then the suppliers. It would become "cost of defense" roulette for everyone unless Judge Acosta intervened. He did not.

However, I said this would not be the same as before. It was not. Sealy hired a good law firm in Los Angeles for its representation. The other nine supplier defendants, all large corporations, hired one law firm... mine. They would split the defense cost nine ways. It would not over burden any one of them or their insurance policies.

As we prepared for the first Pre-Trial Conference after the Master Complaint, we were representing 32 defendants and they touched most of the products and furnishings consumed in the fire. Our client list included Allied Signal, Amoco, E.I. duPont de Nemours & Co., Dow Chemical Company, Firestone Tire & Rubber Company, Foamex International, Georgia-Pacific Corporation, BFGoodrich, Goodyear Tire & Rubber Company, ICI America's, Inc., Monsanto, Occidental Petroleum, Olin Corporation, Quantum, Inc., PPG Industries, Sealed Air Corp., Texaco, Uniroyal, Inc., Union Carbide Co., W.R. Grace Chemical Co., Weyerhaeuser, Inc. and eleven others. They joined together through the auspices of the Chemical Manufacture's Association ("CMA"). By combining all of these mega corporations together we were able to avoid the hardship of the American Rule. The English Rule would have precluded suing them.

Because we would not represent any end product in the building, they each had their own attorneys. There were defense lawyers from New York, Detroit, Atlanta, Boston, Florida, Chicago, Los Angeles and perhaps other states I do not recall, and a large number from San Juan. Further, the idea of a common defense for more than one defendant was taking root. The Liberty Mutual Insurance Company law firm, from Boston, had an excellent lawyer who represented six product suppliers who were insured by Liberty Mutual. We had a terrific group of attorneys, many with significant trial experience. The plaintiffs were in for a fight they had not seen before.

The initial Pre-Trial Conference is significant in Mass Torts. It fashions the procedure for managing and scheduling the case. The plaintiffs had a view to make the case both big — hundreds or perhaps thousands of depositions — and fast. Moreover, everything would be tried at once, making it even bigger and forcing the defendants and their insurers to suffer. We agreed with them, bigger and faster would be fine. We had more joint resources than they did. All we had to do was marshal our resources together, divide up the work and responsibility, and then organize the trial to win.

A scheduling Order was published, as were certain rules for conducting the litigation. All the depositions by both sides would be taken within a six-month period from mid-June to mid-December. This would include full discovery of only selected plaintiffs. To avoid more than 1,000 plaintiffs from testifying, each plaintiff would answer a questionnaire prepared by both sides to detail his or her claims, injuries and damages. In turn, only twelve plaintiffs would be selected to be representative of everyone at trial. Each side would select six and the twelve could be fully deposed. Discovery depositions of the dozens of defendants would proceed as usual. There were seventy-eight defendants going to trial so that was a lot of depositions.

The Order also stated there would be no depositions of any expert witnesses. This was a major departure from prior cases, but also a significant savings. There were expert depositions in the MGM Grand case that lasted weeks, with so many lawyers in attendance. Here, each expert would issue a written Report. If his testimony at trial was at variance with or beyond the scope of his Report, it would be stricken. In some respects, this proved to be beneficial. This was a large savings in costs. Other benefits were also present. For example, the PLC's claim against the glass company, PPG Industries, was novel. Glass does not burn or cause fires. But this fire broke windows so sue someone. The expert witness to support the claim had no litigation experience. He did not testify well at trial.

Finally, the Order prohibited jury research or mock trials to test our defenses on the island of Puerto Rico. Where did this come from?

The Order stated that a Pre-Trial Compliance document would be prepared after discovery closed detailing the evidence you might present at trial, including all discovery. The date would be set later. Moreover, Federal Rules of Civil Procedure 12(b)(6) and 56 were suspended. There would be no pre-trial motions for dismissals allowed. It was amazing. Every other court wanted these motions so peripheral defendants can be dismissed, usually filed by a certain date. They clutter the proceedings. The only rationale I could imagine was that forcing everyone to trial kept everyone's "cost of defense" high and placed risk on the insurers. It not only had to pay for cost of defense for the duration, but also had to pay for a trial, with a risk of loss. That said, we shrugged our shoulders. We saw the plaintiffs' handwriting in this Order. Later we would know how and why. But we came to San Juan for a trial and all our clients were splitting the cost.

Our view was to bring it on, for the first time the "worst" is actually "best." Moreover, soon all the other defendants would be aligned and cooperating, not just our 32-member defense group.

The Chemical Manufacturing group is powerful. I suggested and its leaders foresaw a complete combined defense effort by combining with the insurers of the other defendants. Long story short, through the auspices of the Center for Public Resources in New York, all the insurers were brought together to align with our defense strategy. They did just that. All the other defendants were now aligned with us into a unitary "defense group."

Anticipating potential disagreements with defense strategies, they hired a mediator. He was Bill Champlin, an excellent lawyer from Hartford, Connecticut. He moderated our defense conferences and attended the entire trial. His work was beyond valuable. His decision was final on defense disputes. He held the common defense group together through a number of rough patches. Finally, the Order set the trial to begin in mid-June of 1989.

To sum up the discovery, over five hundred depositions were taken within a six-month period all over the United States and other countries. Attorneys for each defendant defended its discovery. My firm defended each of our clients. For all the witnesses, we employed a simple strategy. Our entire joint defense group sent two lawyers to each deposition; they issued a report at the end of the day. We read the report and forwarded any questions we wanted asked to the two lawyers. The cost savings were immense. Over time, we had six or eight depositions occurring on the same day. Deposition disputes were argued before Judge Arenas, often over the phone. It all went smoothly and there were no ugly surprises. Thereafter, the lengthy expert Reports were prepared and filed.

December of 1988 came, and discovery closed. It was now time to prepare the Pre-Trial Compliance document, which was due in April of 1989. When, where and how? Fortunately, Bally had recently retained Skadden Arps, a large New York law firm, for the defense of its slot machines. They made their offices and resources available to prepare the Compliance. A group of lawyers gathered there and literally worked around the clock. The Plaintiffs' Legal Committee had the same task. In mid-April of 1989, the Compliance by both sides was complete. It consumed twenty-four of the largest binders available. I do not know if anyone ever tried to read it all.

Meanwhile, Judge Acosta had been preparing for the trial. There was no appropriate courtroom in San Juan of sufficient size. There was, however, a relatively new high-rise bank building that was unoccupied above the eighth floor. As a result, the Government Services Administration ("GSA") leased two floors, the ninth and tenth. On the ninth floor it constructed a Document and Evidence Depository. More than 1 million papers and documents were filed, indexed and stored there. In addition, all the exhibits to use at trial and the fire artifacts were also stored there. Clerks behind a counter would find files that we requested, and we would sign for them.

On the tenth floor, GSA built a "courtroom." It more resembled a law school classroom. When you entered, it had tables and chairs aligned in semi-circle tiers around one half of the room. There were seats at the tables for over sixty lawyers. They faced an open area. Behind it was a "bench" as in a courtroom. Judge Acosta would sit there behind it, overlooking the open area, facing the rows of lawyers. In front of him, on the left, was the witness box with a chair. To his right, across the space, was a jury room with a glass wall. The jury would watch the trial through glass windows in a sound sealed room. Immediately to his right behind the bench was a long desk for Judge Arenas and the senior law clerk.

The podium for the speaking lawyer was in the open space facing Judge Acosta, the jury room and the witness chair. As you entered and looked left was a small gallery with about 14 seats. You required a pass to enter it.

For the first time in a federal courthouse, the entire "courtroom" was wired for sound communications and with wall-mounted motorized TV cameras to record the trial. A large console was at the base of Judge Acosta's bench. A technician sat there and controlled the cameras, microphones — everything. The entire trial would be taped by TV. If an attorney needed a question read back or part of the testimony or an argument, he would obtain it from the TV technician on a video tape, which would then be transcribed.

Each lawyer's table had a small console with a switch, a light, and a microphone. If you wanted to make an objection, you pressed a button, and a light would show in front of Judge Acosta as well as at your seat. He would recognize you. You could ask a question with your microphone. You would be invited to come forward to the podium to argue your objection. It would then be ruled on. Meanwhile, the jury in the jury room — who heard the trial proceedings through speakers — would be tuned out. Instead, they heard music playing until the trial resumed.

To enter the courtroom, we received a plastic card with our photo, name, and other information. We showed this ID to the guard at the door and passed through a metal detector. Your briefcase was x-rayed or opened for review.

One of the benefits of the bank building was our ability to rent an entire floor and to put our law firm offices on it. We completely outfitted the 12th floor as an operating law firm office. Moreover, when we went to court, we simply took the elevator down two floors. We parked in the basement of the building, in reserved spaces. If this was the future of lawsuits, we all appreciated the convenience. This was particularly true in the summer months when the heat and humidity in San Juan is oppressive. We enjoyed air-conditioning in a new building.

Now that we had a courthouse, depository and law firm, we secured housing. We rented high-rise condominiums at the beach, as did other lawyers who chose to spend most of their time at trial. Our condominium was a penthouse with four bedrooms, so four of us could live there. We had a great view. It was a twenty-minute drive to the building. With me lived Vic Maddox, as keen a lawyer as you will ever meet. He went to trial daily with me and was our principal trial lawyer. He was respected by all of the plaintiffs' trial lawyers because he had worked with them in the owners' trial. There was also Mike Mercer, who practiced with me for years. He handled all the settlements and insurance issues; he was previously an in-house lawyer for an insurance company. The fourth bedroom was rotational. In another condominium were Elaine Lamlein, my secretary, and a rotating secretary from my law firm. My legal assistant, Cheri Baird, also lived there as did Katie Yunker, a brilliant lawyer and law school professor who signed on for the trial. Katie and Vic Maddox drafted and filed our daily trial motions. If you had an issue at trial requiring the court to rule, you filed your motion by 7:00 p.m. each night. The reply was due by 9:00 p.m. Winston Miller, a long-standing partner of mine and an excellent trial lawyer, was living with Ed Moss in his condo. Winston was my second chair for everything I could not do — which was a lot. Other lawyers from my firm also participated and lived in San Juan for months at a time.

The trial was now looming in two months. We gathered all of our files — boxes and boxes — and trial exhibits in Louisville. We moved everything to our new offices in San Juan. We shared our offices with Ed Moss, who was defending Otis Elevator. Ed is probably the best lawyer I have ever known. He was active in all our meetings and instrumental in our decisions. We used his offices in Miami often for defense meetings in the U.S.

In May of 1989, Magistrate Judge Arenas scheduled a final Pre-Trial Conference to address trial questions and issues. He reviewed the procedures to "work" in the new courtroom. Decorum would be important and enforced. He issued a final Pre-Trial Order. Opening statements would be conducted over four days, two days for each side. We had to schedule time for each defense lawyer. There would be no objections during opening statements. This was curious, indeed. The general rule is that if you do not object to an improper statement, you waive it. While there are usually only a few objections during opening statements at trials, they are important; this appeared to be an open door for abuse. We concluded that Judge Acosta did not want the responsibility to make prompt rulings on objections.

We had a high confidence level that we would win this case, Judge Acosta and his machinations notwithstanding. We felt the plaintiff's lawyers overplayed their hand by suing too many products and companies. Everyone knew cardboard could be burned... so what? In fact, at the trial's opening, the local defense lawyer for a local cardboard supplier, who was in our insurance defense group, made an opening statement. He came forward, introduced himself and his local client to the jury. He said, "My client sold cardboard that was in the hotel." He paused and then sat down. Most of the jurors smiled.

We tested our defenses before mock juries of Puerto Ricans. They were conducted in New York City, not Puerto Rico, the jurors having recently moved there from San Juan. The mock juries confirmed our optimism.

It finally was time to start the trial. An entire book could be written about it. By necessity, this is a long and at times bizarre story. I will condense the thirteen months into two stories.

The San Juan case was the first to address whether testimony, by trial or deposition, could be taken remotely by television. This was challenged by my associates Vic and Katie, including an appeal to the Ninth Circuit Court of Appeals, but was not resolved. So, the cross examination, by a plaintiff's lawyer, of a carpet company owner who lived in Columbia, South Carolina was set for TV. He was being treated for a heart condition so could not appear in San Juan. It was decided that he could testify by closed circuit TV. He would appear at the Federal Courthouse in Columbia, South Carolina, and be sworn in to face a TV camera with his lawyer at his side. The TV signal would be sent by a satellite hookup to our San Juan console and technician. The PLC lawyer at the podium in San Juan would ask questions of the witness in Columbia. We all came to court that morning looking forward to this technical marvel. Remember, it was 1989. This could be amazing.

Court was convened. In the witness chair sat a TV set. The plaintiff's lawyer was at the podium. All the lawyers and jurors were staring at the TV set sitting in the witness chair. The courtroom technician turned on the set. We saw a test pattern. Judge Acosta was talking on the phone to the Columbia courthouse. The witness there was sworn. The proceeding would now begin. The test pattern left the TV screen, it flickered and then produced a picture. It was Deputy Dawg, the cartoon character! Not one lawyer laughed. We were all too afraid to laugh out loud — but the jury did. The satellite hookup was mistakenly connected to the cartoon channel.

By afternoon, the technicalities were fixed. The elderly gentleman appeared on the screen. Questioning began. He not only looked ill, but he also was hard of hearing. Most of the questions had to be repeated or explained. Judge Acosta was flummoxed when his lawyer in Columbia objected. Testimony by TV was a bust and was not used again during the trial.

The second story is quite serious. During the first weeks of the trial, at appropriate times, defense attorneys would object to questions or documents. Judge Acosta would confer with his senior law clerk, Ms. Vilma Vila, and then rule. We rarely won the objection. After trial one afternoon we discussed this. We decided to get the video of the first one hundred objections to review. We reviewed it. Only four objections were sustained, ninety-six were over-ruled. Ms. Vila was active in all of them. There was clear bias for the plaintiffs occurring in this trial.

At our next general meeting of all defense counsel, we

discussed this issue. One of our San Juan attorney's said Ms. Vila was married. Her maiden name was the same as one of the lawyers on the PLC. They were brother and sister. Judge Acosta was conferring with the sister of a PLC member. Was she biased? Did this explain the strange Pre-Trial Orders and all of the adverse rulings? We decided to confront Judge Acosta to remove her from the case. When we asked Judge Acosta, he was indignant, and refused. We now knew how much he was relying on her... totally. Did we have a "plaintiff" in the Judge's chambers for this trial?

After much discussion, we decided to press Judge Acosta to recuse himself from the case for his failure to remove Ms. Vila. At worst she was biased and active, at best she looked improper. A recusal motion is a draconian step. It can be a difficult motion to win because it requires us to prove the misconduct of the judge. That bar is set high. Moreover, the consequences, if you lose, can be a hostile judge for the rest of the trial. We concluded that we already had a hostile environment. How could it be worse? An appointed new and experienced U.S. District Court trial judge from the States would be the answer we needed. Judge Acosta refused to recuse himself. We then filed papers asking the First Circuit Court of Appeals, which oversaw Puerto Rico, to recuse Judge Acosta.

We hired an ethics expert from Yale law school, Jeffry Hazard, as our lawyer. The PLC hired one from Harvard, Arthur Miller. They argued the case in Boston before a three-judge panel that included Stephen Gerald Breyer. He now sits on the Supreme Court of the United States. We lost the recusal motion. Interestingly, there were nine more interlocutory appeals to the First Circuit from San Juan during the trial. They all lost. The First Circuit wanted no part of this strange trial in Puerto Rico.

We returned to the courtroom the next Monday with some apprehension of what to expect. Beware the law of unintended consequences. We learned later that the recusal motion and appeal was very personal and embarrassing to Judge Acosta. He believed that his reputation was being tarnished. He had serious concerns that it might happen again and he would be removed. He, and Ms. Vila, wanted to avoid that if they could. Like turning on a switch, the defense objections and motions were more fairly received. The playing field for the trial became more level.

To sum these 13 months up, as the trial proceeded the plaintiffs' case was organized so the plaintiff's lawyers would attack each product and its supplier group in a sequence. They started with the Sealy sofa bed and its nine-member defense group. We would then defend the individual suppliers. The defenses went well so they would approach us to settle out our defendants for that specific product. The settlement offers were modest and reasonable. By settling, the defendant could avoid the risk of a bad jury verdict like we had in Yonkers. It could close its book on the risk reserve. So, we would settle and the defendant would avoid the risk of a bad verdict but remain in our defense group to share the defense costs.

The PLC took nine months to present their case. We had a three-day break to organize ourselves and start our defense. The consensus was overwhelming that we were winning. We heard a rumor that the PLC had $16 million dollars in loans at a local bank. It was getting nervous and pressing the PLC. By now, we were a solid defense team of eighteen trial lawyers, five from my law firm. We had mutual respect; everyone actively participated. Our San Juan lawyers were watching and studying the jurors throughout the PLC's case. Puerto Ricans are demonstrative people. They do not sit around with "poker faces." The jurors had selected their foreman, a middle-aged businessman. He was particularly demonstrative; he was grimacing at many of the PLC expert witnesses. He did not like their testimony. We decided to truncate our case from as much as six months to less than three months. We wanted to pound home the fault of the hotel for this fire tragedy. Then let the jury decide.

At the conclusion of the trial, but before closing arguments, all of our defendants had settled and been dismissed. But I remained to continue the defense and work on the closing arguments. In every Mass Tort trial I defended, I made an opening statement and closing argument. The few attorneys for the remaining defendants made excellent closing arguments. The jury returned verdicts in their favor. They were all dismissed. Not one of the 78 defendants in our group that went through trial together was found liable for the fire.

Our initial strategies proved successful. Everyone was pleased with the result. The last Chemical Manufacturers meeting was cheerful and rewarding. The entire experience was a treasure box of memories for everyone.

There is no need to review in any detail the litany of aberrations and abuses in our legal system that played out in San Juan. This outrageously excessive litigation speaks for itself: the problems of a politically appointed judge, the American Rule instead of the English Rule requiring the losers to pay our attorney's fees and, most importantly, without contingency fees for the plaintiff's lawyers there would never have been a product liability lawsuit. In the end, the jury of citizens made the correct decision.

At the end of the day, an insurance company estimated the cost of defense to see how it compared to the MGM Grand case. It concluded that the San Juan case, defended through all of the discovery and a thirteen-month trial, produced a total of only $60 million in settlements. The cost (attorneys' fees and expenses) to defend the entire case was $50 million. Another $100 million was recovered but not from the 78 defendants. This was compared to the MGM Grand case seven years earlier. That entire case — without a trial — produced $200 million in settlements and cost $250 million to defend. We had saved over $250 million dollars with a combined, joint defense and a trial. Our initial strategies were vindicated.

There was an "intended consequence" from the case. During the trial, in 1990, a deadly fire occurred at the Happy

Land Social Club in Brooklyn, New York. It was an old, two story building without sprinklers. It was a social club for Hondurans in the city. A spurned lover of the hat check girl returned with two jugs of gasoline purchased at a local Amoco station. He poured them into the club and set a fire. The resulting fire burned up the old, wood paneled stairway to the large room above, where the patrons were dancing. Ninety-five people died and scores were injured.

Lawsuits were filed in Brooklyn, but they were not the same as those in San Juan, MGM Grand or Supper Club. The usual lawyer suspects from those cases were not directly involved. They had learned their lesson.

We did defend one of the Happy Land Social Club defendants, Amoco. We had represented Amoco in San Juan. The defense went well and it was dismissed. As in San Juan, Amoco was innocent; all it did was sell gasoline to a person with a can. We did not know then that thirteen years later The Station nightclub fire in Rhode Island would replicate much of this again.

THE OKLAHOMA CITY BOMBING (1995)

You have now seen much of the mischief that the six aberrations and flaws I describe can cause in Mass Tort lawsuits. However, not every Mass Tort exhibits all of them. The excellent judge in the Air Canada case produced the correct result. One of the more memorable events we remember was the morning we learned of the Oklahoma City bombing tragedy. It became a Mass Tort lawsuit for all the wrong reasons.

At approximately 9:00 a.m. on April 19, 1995, Timothy McVeigh parked his yellow Ryder truck at the curb, directly below the daycare center at the Alfred P. Murrah Federal Building in Oklahoma City. Contained within the van were 7,000+ pounds of explosive materials, including about 5,000 pounds of oil-mixed ammonium nitrate fertilizer with 500 blasting caps to detonate it. He lit the fuse and fled the truck, driving away in his car parked nearby. It was an immense and malevolent bomb he had methodically constructed at the farm of Terry Nichols.

At 9:02 a.m., the bomb detonated. It destroyed one-third of the front of the eleven-floor concrete building. The blast killed 168 of the 640 occupants in the building — including 19 children in the daycare center.[28] It injured many more, hospitalizing more than 650. It impacted a sixteen-block radius of the city and damaged hundreds of buildings. The blast was recorded 53 miles away. It was the worst terrorist attack on our soil in American history prior to the 9/11 attack on the World Trade Center. Much has been reported about the tragic attack, the arrests of McVeigh and Nichols,

[28] Oklahoma City Bombing, History (August 21, 2018). Retrieved from https://www.history.com/topics/1990s/oklahoma-city-bombing.

McVeigh's trial and subsequent execution.

Less than a month after the event, Johnnie Cochran, the Los Angeles lawyer famous for the O.J. Simpson murder trial defense, joined with a plaintiff's law firm in Oklahoma City. They filed a contingency fee, class action lawsuit on behalf of all of the victims for more than $1 billion dollars. They sued ICI PLC ("ICI"), the English company that was accused of making the fertilizer Terry Nichols purchased at a Kansas farm co-op to produce the bomb. They were seeking a jury trial. The suit alleged, in essence, that the fertilizer was inherently unsafe because it was easily made into a massively explosive bomb. Therefore, they averred, it was an unreasonably dangerous product under the law. Similar lawsuits were also filed in Houston, Texas.

Ammonium Nitrate ("AN"), invented in Germany in the 1930s, is a remarkable chemical product.[29] It is an "oxidizer," meaning that when it dissolves, it freely releases nitrogen and oxygen. Thus, it is a perfect fertilizer when made into the hard round "prills" the size of aspirin tablets and distributed by large farm fertilizer spreaders. It does not turn to powder in the spreader but instead settles intact on the soil and then dissolves. It is estimated that because AN is inexpensive and so useful, 40 percent of the world population would not be fed today but for ammonium nitrate.[30]

When made into softer absorbent prills, mixed precisely with fuel oil at the site and then detonated, it is a perfect explosive. AN, when used as an explosive, is largely responsible for building the interstate highway system throughout America. As an explosive, it replaced TNT and nitroglycerin because of its safe transportation and handling

---

[29] Tim Harford, How fertiliser helped feed the world, BBC News (January 2, 2017). Retrieved fromhttps://www.bbc.com/news/business-38305504

[30] *Id.*

characteristics. It is non-explosive until mixed with oil and forced to detonate.

At first blush, the filing of such a lawsuit strains credibility. But Mr. Cochran had in mind using several of America's legal abuses in combination.

Why did Johnnie Cochran file such a lawsuit against the most widely used fertilizer in the world? Because he could file the lawsuit without financial punishment. If he loses, he owes the defendant nothing. Remember, there is no English Rule in America.

He filed a class action lawsuit to have all the hundreds of plaintiffs combined into one large claim. This was intended to present a massive claim — more than $1 billion dollars — to strike terror into ICI, the English defendant and its insurers.

He asked for a jury trial in Oklahoma City, seeking damages from a foreign company. Could this be "home cooking" made manifest? Could Oklahoma citizens turn away their devastated fellow citizens and their estates in favor of a foreign corporation? He filed the lawsuit in state court before an elected Oklahoma City circuit judge.

I was interviewed by ICI twice, first in the U.S. and second in London. My law firm was retained for the defense. We began by addressing the local judge and state court issue. We preferred to have the case in federal court rather than state court. By statute, foreign companies can gain access to the federal courts for their lawsuits. This was intended to prevent them from being subjected to local biases. So, we successfully applied to have the case removed and transferred to federal court. Fortunately, the removed case was assigned to an excellent United States District Court Judge who had been a U.S. Attorney for Oklahoma City. He was appointed by President George W. Bush. His criminal prosecution background prepared him to see McVeigh and Nichols for what they were, heinous criminals. We had the good fortune of a quality judge.

After all, the AN fertilizer did exactly what it was designed to do when mixed with fuel oil and heavily detonated. It blew up, just as it had been blowing up since the 1930s. The fertilizer can be made explosive. It often is, especially by farmers removing tree stumps. Moreover, the fertilizer was expressly repurposed and misused by terrorists. The fertilizer did not make the bomb — terrorists did. All the fault for the tragedy lay with them, end of story.

The terrorist attack was an unprecedented event, so the lawsuit presented unique circumstances and novel legal issues. Fertilizer is used and sold all over the globe. To give the plaintiffs every chance to prove their case, the court opened worldwide discovery against the English company. This included more than a dozen countries so the plaintiff's lawyers could look for anything to hang their hat on. These countries included Argentina, Chile, Mexico, Australia, South Africa, India, China, Ireland and, of course, the U.S. and Britain. We were forced to send lawyers to each country, some for weeks, where ICI had an ammonium nitrate business. This was not a problem for me however, because none of my associates ever complained of the chance to travel abroad. In the end, all of the tens of thousands of documents that were produced and reviewed amounted to a hill of beans in support of the plaintiff's case. Because we retained experts to recreate the bomb and shared it with the FBI and Scotland Yard, they shared technical support with us for the defense. All of this work meant that the defense would be costly. But ICI was steadfast that they had done nothing wrong. There would be no cost of defense settlement although the plaintiff's lawyers kept probing for one.

After providing all the discovery, we filed an extensive "speaking" Federal Rule 12(b)(6) Motion to Dismiss. This resembles the summary judgment motions I described earlier in Yonkers and Air Canada. Our legal briefs were extensive. The Federal Court granted our motion, dismissing all the claims and lawsuits. Judge David Lynn Russell wrote a 49-page opinion. He found that McVeigh's use of fertilizer to construct his terrorist bomb was an unforeseeable misuse of the product, an intervening, superseding cause, overwhelming and negating all the plaintiffs' claims. The dismissal was appealed. The Tenth Circuit Court of Appeals, writing a 56-page opinion after oral arguments, affirmed the dismissal. That appellate decision established the legal foundation in American law for lawsuits arising from terrorist attacks. It became significant for the defense of some of the lawsuits filed after the World Trade Center terrorist disaster.

At the end of the day, Mr. Cochran's effort to misuse the United States civil tort system to his advantage failed. With Judge Russell on the case, justice was done. But that does not justify Mr. Cochran's lawsuit. It should never have been filed.

There is an interesting aside to this example. The English company was the fourth largest chemical company in the world, after Dow Chemical, DuPont de Nemours and BASF. It was a revered company in London and because of its large size and impeccable record, it was known as the "Queen's Company." After I was retained to lead the defense, I was flown to London to meet the ICI Board at a special meeting to review the claims and lawsuits. They were distinguished members of both London's corporate world and government. For openers, they were quite upset that they should be accused of fostering the terrorist attack in the United States. They were deeply concerned and wishing for an explanation as to how such a lawsuit could be filed in the United States at all, as such a suit would never be permitted in London. It was a lively and animated meeting and required my explanation of how America had so corrupted English law as to even allow this lawsuit. Hence, the meeting lasted nearly twice as long as the allotted time. My assurances to them that our defenses would prevail were proven out over the following meetings held on a quarterly basis.

Throughout the defense, the esteemed General Counsel of the company, Victor White, provided unstinting support for our strategies. Over time, he and I developed a working relationship and friendship. When we won the case, I called him to advise that Judge Russell had dismissed the case and that I appreciated his support throughout. His only comment was: "Carl, it is always easy to take good advice." I love the English! End of story.

"CITIZEN JURY" OF YOUR PEERS

The United States is unique among the civilized world by mandating jury trials in civil cases. Specifically, the Seventh Amendment to United States Constitution provides:

> *In suits at common law, where the value in controversy shall exceed twenty dollars, the right to trial by jury shall be preserved, and no fact tried by jury shall be otherwise re-examined in any Court in the United States than according to the rules of common law.*

While this amendment governs only federal cases, it has been adopted by every state but one for non-federal cases. Thus, it requires jury trials in all civil cases in the United States. In other countries, this is rare, indeed.

What does a jury trial mean? In England, the right to jury trial was established by the Magna Carta of 1215. Article 29 states:

> *No freeman is to be taken or imprisoned or disseised of his free tenement or of his liberties or free customs, or outlawed or exiled or in any way ruined, nor will we go against such a man or send against him save by lawful judgement of his peers or by the law of the land. To no-one will we sell or deny of delay right or justice.*

Under English law the jury was selected from "peers" *i.e.*, people like yourself. The idea of a jury of peers was adopted by America's Founding Fathers when drafting the Constitution. The operative word for selection to be on a peer jury is "citizen." The panel of jurors is selected from the voting rolls of the U.S. citizens in the community.

When our Founding Fathers created the United States

Constitution, they believed the people should decide legal disputes, not a king. They were, in fact, inventing a democracy for citizens. But when making something this important with a limitless future, "beware the law of unintended consequences." It was impossible for them to foresee all the changes that would take place over the following 240 plus years. Further, their focus was not on a civil law system or the judges and citizen juries that would implement it. The most important decision, jury trial by citizens, seemed perfectly suited for the revolutionary times.

To put this in context, at that time 240 years ago, only the white male landowners of America could vote as citizens. Thus, the other Americans including women, tenants, slaves, Indians and indentured servants were not citizens. So, juries would be composed of "citizens" identical to the Founders themselves, no one else. Who better to resolve their disputes? For instance, if a neighbor's cattle broke through his fence and damaged his crops, let like-minded men decide the case. Was the fence poorly constructed or did a lightning and thunderstorm (Act of God defense) cause the stampede? Or let us consider that a wagon has a shaky wheel, so the owner takes it to a blacksmith to be fixed. While driving back home, the repaired wheel collapses, injuring the owner's leg and ruining the goods he just purchased from the market. Did the blacksmith do a bad job (negligence), was the wheel itself defective (product liability standard of care) or did the owner drive too fast going over ruts in the road (his fault)? White male landowning citizens will decide these claims. Lastly, what if someone buys a horse from another and relies on the seller's assurances of the quality and soundness of the animal; can the buyer sue when the horse founders? Because the claim depends on what was said and relied on at the time of sale and what a reasonable buyer should have seen and examined, who better to decide these issues than like-minded land and horse owning white male citizens? While this may appear logical in that long ago day and age, "beware of the law of unintended consequences."

Over the ensuing 240 years, myriad changes occurred in American society. But the narrowly conceived rule of civil trials by juries of "citizens from your community" remained constant. To the possible dismay of the white land-owning Founding Fathers, if they should visit America today, the term "citizen" has been expanded to now include women, African Americans and all voters born in America regardless of land ownership. In fact, if you visit your local courthouse to watch a civil trial, you will see that white male landowners are now in the minority on the jury, if they are present at all.

Why is the civil jury of United States citizens such a problem to the American system of justice? The first answer is the definition of "your peers" for jury selection in the American legal system.

I recently gave a presentation to a group of retina surgeons. Retina surgeons are among the smartest, most educated, and best trained doctors in the medical community. They perform delicate, precise, difficult and time-consuming surgeries in the most obscure areas of the eye. I had macular degeneration surgery that prevented me from going blind. I know first-hand, and greatly appreciate, what these skilled surgeons can do.

Let us consider a hypothetical lawsuit as an example involving a claim against a retina surgeon. A farmer's wife — we will name her Mary — notices she is losing vision in her eye, but she is reluctant to seek medical help. Finally, her husband gets her to a doctor who then refers her to a major hospital where retina surgery is performed. Her surgeon discovers she has both a detached retina and macular degeneration. She may have waited too long, so the chances of successful surgery and saving the sight of the eye are poor. But better to try surgery than do nothing. The surgeon performs the surgery but is unsuccessful. The disease is too advanced so the eyesight could not be saved.

Sometime later, Mary is at a church luncheon, wearing an eye patch. A lawyer at the luncheon notices Mary's eye patch.

After some discussion, he talks Mary into suing the eye surgeon for medical malpractice for not saving the eye. She will owe him nothing if they lose. He takes the case for a 40 percent fee, meaning he will receive 40 percent of whatever Mary is awarded as a result of the lawsuit. He then hires a less competent, small practice eye doctor for a handsome fee to criticize the surgery performed by the retina surgeon. He has created a medical malpractice case to take to trial. The testimony of malfeasance surgery by the lawyer's hired doctor witness creates an issue of fact for the jury to decide at trial.

At the trial, the jury will be composed of ordinary citizens from the community, Mary's "peers," but they are not "peers" of the retina surgeon. There will be no retina surgeons on the jury to understand the difficult specifics of the case and the complications and technicalities of what actually had to be overcome during the surgery. There may be no one with any medical background on the jury at all. People like Mary, not the surgeon, will decide the case as Mary sits at the Plaintiffs table with an eye patch over a sightless eye. Thus, the retina surgeon's chances for a successful jury trial in this case are not high. The jury is stacked in Mary's favor, not his. This explains why 94 percent of medical malpractice lawsuits in America are settled and not taken to trial before a jury. There are no doctor peer juries. In fact, if the jury had been composed of retina surgeons, the plaintiff's attorney would have dismissed his case.

Other similar examples of citizen juries trying complex and technically difficult cases are everywhere. Recently, two of them involved common, and useful products. In St. Louis, a lawsuit was filed against Johnson & Johnson to recover damages from using talcum powder, an ingredient found in baby powder, alleging that it caused ovarian cancer.[31] Despite United States governmental agencies finding the product to be safe and it having been used by millions of women and babies for over 100 years, the jury awarded $4.6 billion to the plaintiffs. In another lawsuit brought in San Francisco, a jury awarded a school groundskeeper $289 million after concluding that his terminal cancer was caused by the weed killer Roundup, one of the most popular and useful weed killers on the worldwide market.[32] Monsanto's (Roundup's manufacturer) evidence consisted of more than 800 scientific studies and reviews, which found that the ingredients found in Roundup did not cause the Plaintiff's cancer. The results of these two trials became severe problems for Johnson & Johnson and Monsanto, as you will see later.

There is another factor that often influences citizen juries when the defendant is a corporation — the distrust in America of large corporations. This arises from a number of causes. People feel remote from corporations because they appear impersonal and focused only on their bottom-line profits. People believe corporations will do anything for profits, including selling them faulty products, and they never apologize for what they do. The news cycle in America regularly reports on illegal or abusive corporate behavior.

---

[31] Robert Patrick and Joel Currier, Talc Cancer verdict of $4.6 billion from St. Louis jury sends 'very powerful message', *St. Louis Today: St. Louis Post- Dispatch* (July 13, 2018). Retrieved from https://www.stltoday.com/news/local/crime-and-courts/talc-cancer-verdict-of-billion-from-st-louis-jury-sends/article_c15e7f98-fce0-5a74-80ee-45371d5e98b1.html.

[32] Mike James and Jorge L. Ortiz, Jury orders Monsanto to pay $289 million to cancer patient in Roundup lawsuit, USA TODAY (August 10, 2018). Retrieved from https://www.usatoday.com/story/news/2018/08/10/jury-orders-monsanto-pay-289-million-cancer-patient-roundup-lawsuit/962297002/.

While there are such instances, they do not accurately reflect the conduct of all corporations. There are two million corporations in America. Only a very few are the bad apples in that barrel. However, media reports of good behavior are rare.

In addition, the general view is that the Chief Executive Officer ("CEO") of a corporation makes too much money. *This is true!* The spread between the salary of the corporate CEO and the workers, who are laboring to make the products sold by the company, is the biggest it has ever been, on average 361 times larger for the CEO than the average worker.[33] According to a recent *New York Times* article, the Economic Policy Institute reports that from 1978 to 2019 compensation for the typical worker grew 14 percent but for CEOs it grew 1,167 percent. The money in America is being given to CEOs. Despite the public backlash, these numbers continue to grow larger.

All of this explains why the targets of large lawsuits are often corporations. Nearly 90 percent of U.S. corporations are involved in some sort of litigation, and the average company maintains approximately 37 cases at a time.[34]

Moreover, juries can relate to the Plaintiff in a suit against a corporation. Most people have had one or more bad experiences in their lives at the hands of a corporate entity. As a result, the additional element of emotion is added to the jury's perceptions. People are mad about the uneven distribution of power between corporations and themselves.

---

[33] Diana Hembree, CEO Pay Skyrockets To 361 Times That of The Average Worker, *Forbes* (May 22, 2018), Retrieved from https://www.forbes.com/sites/dianahembree/2018/05/22/ceo-pay-skyrockets-to-361-times-that-of-the-average-worker/#15b27068776d.

[34] Nearly 90 percent of U.S. Corporations Juggle Multiple Lawsuits, *Insurance Journal* (November 7, 2005). Retrieved from https://www.insurancejournal.com/magazines/mag-features/2005/11/07/62341.htm

Sitting on a jury in a Tort trial against a large corporation provides the perfect opportunity to get even by making it pay.

There is no reason to believe this bias will abate or reverse anytime soon, as the unequal income distribution and bad conduct reporting continues to grow. At the end of the day, corporate America can only withstand so many wrong verdicts. Ultimately, they will overwhelm their profits, along with the insurance policies they buy for protection. This is a slippery slope, indeed.

In order to select a fair jury when dealing with the innate distaste of some jurors for corporations (defendants) and what can be the inborn sympathy for the perceived underdogs (plaintiffs), the selection of a jury by a trial lawyer is always a critical task. The outcome of the trial is jury dependent.

At the beginning of the trial, the court provides a large panel of prospective jurors. Of these prospective jurors, depending on the court, usually twelve or six jurors constitute the jury in a civil trial. Because the Constitution gives juries such great power to decide all fact issues and the extent of damages, their selection is the most important part of the trial. On TV, it is cross examination, but in real life it is the jury selection.

So, how are jurors selected? The panel of prospective jurors, which consists of dozens of voters, is randomly selected from the community. They appear at the courthouse. The judge brings a chosen number of them into his courtroom. The prospective jurors may fill out personal questionnaires giving information about education, employment, marital status, etc. If the trial presents unusual issues, there may be questions in that area as well. The questionnaires are designed by the judge in collaboration with the attorneys.

Each attorney gets an opportunity to question the panel of prospective jurors. This process is referred to as *voir dire*. The judge actively oversees and participates. If a juror's response to a question indicates a prejudice, the attorney can move to strike that juror from the panel. If successful, the judge excuses that juror. A final panel is then selected, and each attorney gets to strike a certain number of the panel members (often three). At the end of the process, a jury is selected and seated in the jury box. In large trials, alternate jurors may also be seated to replace a juror who during the trial for some reason can no longer serve.

Because the role of the jury is so important, there are consultants that trial attorneys hire to help them with the jury selection. They assist in drafting *voir dire* questions and observe the answers by the jury panel looking for clues of any bias. The role of jury consultant began in the 1970s by Dr. Donald E. Vincent, the "founding father" of the jury trial consulting industry. He was a brilliant and insightful psychology professor at the University of Southern California in Los Angeles. His first case was for IBM in a large trial in Chicago. His second case was alongside me in the Supper Club trial. Dr. Vincent's participation was valuable in guiding the jury selection and in designing our strategies and evidence for the trial. We won our trial. So did IBM.

I am pleased to say that I worked with Dr. Vincent and his group often. I found his advice to be spot on and wise. He spawned a large industry of look-alikes. There are hundreds of jury consultants at work today. There is even a TV show, "Bull," built around this business. Few significant cases go to trial without a jury consultant for each side. The role of the citizen jury is so important that a trial attorney will leave no stone unturned so he can present his best and most convincing case to his selected jurors; he expects they will favorably receive and accept it.

Nevertheless, a jury is unpredictable, and when emotion and bias mix with a lack of expertise, the outcome can be a perversion of our legal system. One of my cases in particular, described in the next chapter, shows the potential burdens presented by our jury system.

HEALTH MANAGEMENT ORGANIZATIONS (HMOs) (1996-2000)

We are all familiar with Medicare, HMOs and health insurance. The HMOs ran into trouble with their changes in medical coverage years ago. The following provides us with an example of how our civil jury system impacts U.S. litigation.

In the 1990s, the cost of medicine was accelerating at an alarming double-digit rate in the United States. The problem was vexing. In response, Health Management Organizations ("HMO") who provided medical insurance to millions of people, decided to take steps to help bring the cost under control. They added a "medical necessity" provision to the coverage for insurance. The major HMOs — United, Aetna, Kaiser Permanente and Humana — all adopted this new standard of care. Anyone requesting a medical procedure to be covered by his HMO must establish that it is "medically necessary." As a result, medical procedures that had been covered in prior years were now being denied. This left the insured with two choices: Forego the treatment or pay for it themselves. This change was put into effect across the country.

Within each HMO was a medical team of doctors that reviewed each case for "medical necessity." They either approved or denied the coverage requested. There was also a lawyer that would perform a "triage" of the claim if the denial were appealed. Often, the insured was denied the treatment unless the "medical necessity" changed for the worse in the future.

A third choice soon emerged. Hire a lawyer to sue the HMO to pay for the medical treatment and seek damages for the HMO's denial of coverage. Now the anger of the public over new denials of treatment began to surface. In the mid-

1990s, jury verdicts against HMOs started occurring. The verdicts required the HMO to pay for the treatment and assessed millions of dollars in damages for the alleged wrongful denials. In Chicago, a jury assessed millions against United. In Dallas, a jury assessed millions against Aetna. In San Francisco, a jury assessed millions against Kaiser Permanente.

In Louisville, a middle-aged woman sought a hysterectomy. Her surgeon scheduled the surgery. Her insurer, Humana, determined it was not "medically necessary" — which was true. There was no disease present. She simply reached a point in her life where she wanted the surgery. She went forward with the surgery, paying for it herself. Afterwards, she sued Humana for reimbursement, including consequential and punitive damages for the denial. At the end of the trial, the jury returned a verdict in excess of $7 million. That jury, and the public, believed that the insurance should have covered the surgery regardless of "medical necessity."

The HMO industry was under siege. The general public, who composed the "citizen juries," was angry. More lawsuits were being filed for insurance coverage denials. Was there a tipping point in the U.S. where the HMO industry would collapse from excessive verdicts?

My law office was across the street from Humana's headquarters in Louisville, Kentucky. Within a week, I was sitting in a Humana conference room meeting with Humana's directors, officers and lawyers addressing the problem. Over the next week, we began preparing to defend and control the pending lawsuits.

One afternoon, while working at Humana, Michael Moore, author, filmmaker, and activist, appeared at the front door of Humana's headquarters. He brought with him two caskets and a horde of reporters. Cameras were rolling as he attacked Humana for its "heartless" insurance denials. He was calling for Humana's executives to appear and defend themselves.

We discussed what to do. There was a brisk argument. Humana's public relations team, in-house lawyer and CEO were upset at the outrageousness of Mr. Moore's actions. They wanted to confront him, call the police and have him removed from the front of their building. I advised against this. Arresting Mr. Moore would be difficult — he was on the public sidewalk and he did not block the ingress into or egress out of the building. Moreover, if the police were involved, the TV coverage would play badly and be broadcast nationally on the evening news. Most of the public agreed with Michael Moore — not Humana. Confronting him with a Humana spokesperson was also a bad option. Humana had every right to deny coverage for unnecessary medical procedures but a public debate about it with Mr. Moore was doomed from the start. His approach is confrontational. He does not allow discourse and he will talk over whatever you are saying. He is a master of this tactic. Consequently, we decided to wait him out. After about two hours, the press and TV stations lost interest and left. Then Mr. Moore packed up his empty coffins and departed as well. The news coverage was minimal everywhere except in Louisville. Nevertheless, that event described the public's reaction to the new HMO's attempt to bring healthcare costs under control.

Now we had the task of working our way through the pending lawsuits. That will provide an insightful look at the "citizen jury" problem in America.

Aetna, United, Humana and Kaiser Permanente had excellent trial lawyers defend them in Dallas, Chicago, Louisville and San Francisco, but they were unsuccessful. Over $36 million dollars in verdicts caught our attention. What defense would work with a public angry over medical insurance denials?

Humana had cases pending in Florida. One in Tampa appeared ripe for mock jury research and testing. There, an elderly, diabetic patient with advanced ulcers on his leg was being treated in a hospital. He had Humana insurance. His doctor prescribed a "decubitus" mattress for his hospital bed. A decubitus mattress relieves the pressure on the leg laying on the mattress, reducing weight on the ulcers and hopefully allowing them to heal. This requested mattress cost over $800.00. Humana provided a decubitus mattress they considered to be the equivalent; it cost $600.00. The patient's ulcers worsened and eventually the leg required amputation. He then sued Humana for its failure to provide the $800 mattress over the $600 one. How could a $200 cost difference make such a significant difference in a mattress?

We retained two medical experts to testify that the patient was a diabetic and his leg was badly infected with ulcers and could not be saved. Further, the difference between the mattresses was merely cost, otherwise, there was no appreciable difference. The mattress was not the cause of the ulcer deterioration and consequent amputation. On the other side, the plaintiff's doctor stated that he believed he was treating and saving the leg and the mattress change by Humana made a critical difference. We now had a difference of medical opinions. The opinions would be "facts" at a jury trial. So, a "citizen jury" would decide which medical opinion to believe. Who is correct? We had a real claim and defense to test.

We retained a jury consulting firm and scheduled a mock trial. We impaneled 32 Tampa residents to serve as "citizen jurors" to hear and decide our respective cases. We would observe their deliberations through closed circuit TV. We began at 9:00 a.m. By noon, my law partner Greg Belzley and I had each presented our opposing cases in 45-minute presentations which included appropriate exhibits and poster boards. After lunch, the panel was divided into three juries and sent to separate rooms to deliberate and return verdicts. Each jury group had a facilitator to help keep them on track. We observed them on the closed-circuit TV.

To my surprise all three mock juries reached a verdict against Humana relatively quickly. Many of the jurors cited recent events with friends and family members where medical coverage had been denied. They believed that the denial was wrong in their personal experiences and that it was wrong now. Humana must pay damages for changing the mattress. It was now interesting to witness their deliberations regarding the amount Humana should pay in damages for this "wrong." One mock juror believed $600 million was the "right amount." Another mock juror stated that "$200 million was right." After all, Humana was big and rich. In the end, Humana lost the case with all three mock juries; the damages from each mock jury exceeded $30 million. A large sum, indeed, for a $200 difference in mattresses.

This example demonstrates graphically the fundamental problem of the U.S. system of "citizen juries." I submit that if this same case were presented to ten judges, as it would be in England, at least nine of them would dismiss the lawsuit outright. The amputation was medically inevitable and the substitution of one decubitus mattress over another is only a matter of cost, not the effectiveness of either mattress in this case. After all, a less expensive car will drive you down the road just as well as a Cadillac. One just costs more than the other. Humana had done nothing wrong.

We did further mock jury research in both Jacksonville and Ft. Lauderdale for pending cases. These cases were more problematic than the one in Tampa. They more resembled the non-medical necessity claim in Louisville. In the process, in each case I observed mock jurors' express anger at the insurance denials.

Over time, we altered the defense to change the main focus from the medically correct actions of Humana. The small story was that Humana did not deny coverage for treatment, it denied coverage for unnecessary treatment. The large story for the jury focused on the spiraling, out of control costs of healthcare in the U.S. — costs that demanded a solution that all Americans had to financially share. The result from this approach was that much of the rage dissipated. Jurors could see the big picture — not just the small one in the pending case — and became much more understanding and reasonable. Thus, Humana now had a chance to present a case at trial that could be decided more fairly. That said, Humana never got the opportunity to select a jury of "its" peers, HMOs. Rather, the citizen juries were always heavily weighted to a panel of the plaintiff's peers. Therein lies the problem for corporations with the U.S. judicial system and jury trials.

The case of the Tampa patient was settled confidentially. We did not want to chum the litigation waters. We could now buy our peace with more reasonable settlements elsewhere because we believed we could defend, at least to some extent, Humana at trial. Even so, we knew that settlements were better than jury trials. The new defense in Florida that appeared to offer some success with mock juries was shared with the other HMO lawyers at a group conference in Chicago. Over time, all the pending HMO lawsuits were settled, and only a few "runaway" verdicts occurred.

In addition, changes in insurance coverage modifying medical necessity and the healthcare system in the U.S. reduced the escalating costs somewhat. Nevertheless, the problems with citizen juries remain and persist today. Our mock jury research was a graphic example of how citizen juries view corporations in litigation in America.

CLASS ACTION LAWSUITS

Class action lawsuits contribute a great deal to the problems within the United States civil justice system. They are often abused when they are employed by plaintiff's lawyers to expand the size of a simple lawsuit. You will see demonstrated clearly in the case that follows an explanation of how class actions work.

A class action is a civil lawsuit where a plaintiff may file suit as a representative of other members of his class (or group) with the same claim.[35] This occurs where the members of the class are numerous, questions of law and fact are common, the claims or defenses are typical, and the representative party will fairly and accurately protect the interests of the entire class. One common type of class action is a lawsuit brought by the shareholders of a corporation. Because all shareholders own an identical interest in the corporation, if the corporation has wronged one shareholder, it has wronged all shareholders. It would be unequitable for one shareholder to reap all the damages the corporation owes to the exclusion of the others. All the shareholders have the same interest, and the corporation wants them all included in a single proceeding. This is not only common sense but also judicial economy. It allows courts to address the claims of hundreds of similar plaintiffs at once.[36] Many Mass Torts become class actions.

The concept of a class action derives from English common law. In 1820, English courts recognized that all necessary

---

[35] Arthur R. Miller, The Pretrial Rush to Judgment: Are the "Litigation Explosion," "Liability Crisis," and Efficiency Clichés Eroding Our Day in Court and Jury Trial Commitments?, 78 N.Y.U.L. Rev. 982, 997 (2003).
[36] *Id.*

parties to a single claim should be joined together. This idea came to the United States in 1842 when the Supreme Court enacted Equity Rule 48. Equity Rule 48, "officially recogniz[ed] representative suits where the parties were too numerous to be conveniently brought before the court[.]"[37] Eventually, the ability to file class actions was codified in the Federal Rules of Civil Procedure [38] — the official rules that dictate the procedural requirements for civil lawsuits. There the requisites for class certification are detailed. [39]

Throughout this long history, until today, the U.S. has been the most aggressive country to expand the use and coverage of class actions. What started as an attempt to streamline the judicial process quickly became an additional obstacle for courts to overcome.

Class actions became the money-making machine for plaintiffs' attorneys to earn huge sums of money, because of contingency fees, in a relatively short period of time.[40] When similar claims are consolidated into a single lawsuit, all the plaintiffs' claims are resolved simultaneously resulting in a quicker resolution than if the claims were brought individually. Moreover, a class action combines the damages sought from each plaintiff in the class, which results in a massive payout by the defendant.[41] This encourages defendants to rush into a cost of defense settlement, even if they are innocent, simply because the potential claim for

---

[37] In re Joint Eastern & Southern Dist. Asbestos Litigation, 129 B.R. 710, 803 (E.D.N.Y. 1991), judgment vacated, 982 F.2d 721 (2d Cir. 1992).

[38] *See generally* Fed. R. Civ. P. 23.

[39] *id.*

[40] *See* Anthony J. Sebok, *What Do We Talk About When We Talk About Mass Torts?*, 106 Mich. L. Rev. 1213, 1214 (2008).

[41] *See* Anthony J. Sebok, *What Do We Talk About When We Talk About Mass Torts?*, 106 Mich. L. Rev. 1213, 1218–19 (2008).

damages is so large.[42] A defendant that makes a cost of defense settlement in a class action settles the entire litigation. In essence, the defendant has been forced to buy its peace without the full opportunity to defend its innocence.

The application of class actions to Mass Tort lawsuits is more complicated and controversial due to problems associated with class certification. When are the claims too numerous? When are all claims identical? When are the claims or defenses both common and typical? Different parties can look at these issues differently. From the plaintiffs' point of view, a Mass Tort should be a class action. Then all the plaintiffs' claims can be consolidated and combined into a single lawsuit. To the contrary, when multiple claims are involved, in the absence of class action certification, each plaintiff must prove his own claim and his resulting damages. This is a heavy and cumbersome burden on plaintiff's lawyers.

But this can cut both ways. When the judge certifies a class action, that means the class representative speaks for all of the claimants. Thus, a defendant that makes a cost of defense settlement in a class action settles the entire litigation. Once the judge approves the settlement, which is usually, but not always, perfunctory, the defendant has purchased its peace. The settlement and dismissal of one plaintiff is a settlement and dismissal for all.

To give you an idea of the range of Class Actions in the U.S., I reviewed four issues of the publication "Class Action.org Newsletter" published between June 27, 2019 and August 6, 2019. It provides a current listing of Class Actions. Among the numerous pending and potential Class Action lawsuits and claims are the following: travel insurance, NuCO2 carbonated beverage, auto credit unions, bottled water, bird food, text messages (many), refrigerators, SUVs, tires, microwave drawers, dog food, ginger ale, washing

[42] *id.*

machines, candy, soap, spam, massages, credit cards and Nabi tablets. This superficial review covers roughly six weeks. Doing the math indicates that in a year of 52 such weeks, an expansion of nine times will occur in this number. That would suggest more than 200 "products" will have Class Actions filed against them each year. Often the settlements distributed to the Class Action members are only a few dollars. But a class member may be required to complete a host of papers and mailings to recover that small amount. Meanwhile, the Class Action lawyers rake in millions on the cases.

SILICONE BREAST IMPLANTS (1992-2007)

Most Mass Torts arise from product liability lawsuits where often thousands of plaintiffs are alleged to be injured by defectively made products. These cases can go on for years because of their size. Often these suits arise from medical products. The litigation over silicone breast implants is an example, and an embarrassment. It presents every one of the six aberrations, in excess.

For many years, the breast implant of choice was made of silicone. Silicone is an inert jell that can hold its molded form.[43] When implanted in a breast, it appears life-like. It is soft but firm to touch and women are relieved and satisfied when silicone is used for their breast implants.

What began as a single lawsuit with a million-dollar verdict in San Francisco in 1991, involving a claim for an imaginary "autoimmune disease" allegedly caused by a silicone breast implant, evolved into a full-on storm of federal and state court litigation. The storm created a tsunami in 1992 when a successful plaintiff's lawyer recovered another multi-million-dollar verdict. He then went public. Talk show host Phil Donohue, the long-running CBS TV news show *60 Minutes*, and TV journalist Connie Chung came forward to support the claim for the non-existent disease. Not one of them ever mentioned any "medical science" that supported the claims because there was none. As a result, Congress held hearings, but the only three doctors who testified were paid by plaintiff's lawyers; only the fears were presented. The truth was not. The claims and resulting lawsuits were created by an

---

[43] Breast Augmentation Augmentation Mammaplasty, American Society of Plastic Surgeons (2019). Retrieved from https://www.plasticsurgery.org/cosmetic-procedures/breast-augmentation/implants

anecdotal opinion of a fringe pathologist.

Exactly what was this "autoimmune disease" mysteriously discovered by this California pathologist? What were its symptoms? A plaintiff's lawyer was asked this question by the press. He responded that "autoimmune disease" had "flu like symptoms." So, if she had silicone implants, she could develop a headache, upset stomach, fatigue, and perhaps some aches and pains. What if a woman without silicone implants had one or more of these same symptoms? What was causing her alleged "autoimmune disease?" The medical community would answer this question over the next 15 years.

Thousands of new lawsuits were then filed across the country. A class action for all implanted women, hundreds of thousands of them, was filed in Cincinnati, Ohio. Under federal practice rules, when lawsuits over the same subject matter are filed in numerous district courts, they are referred to a single judge. Thus, judicial economy will govern the proceeding, plus the possibility of different results from different judges will be avoided. All of the pending federal lawsuits were consolidated in a single proceeding before a judge in Birmingham, Alabama. You will recall this was also done in the MGM Grand and Air Canada litigations. The state lawsuits proceeded independently.

The lawsuits were now being driven largely by a cabal of powerful plaintiff's lawyers, combined with an array of plastic surgeons. Given a choice of either co-operating with the lawyers by sending them patients or being added as a defendant to the litigation, the plastic surgeons chose the lawyers. One doctor in Nevada referred 9,000 patients to the lawyers. The feeding frenzy was in full bloom. The rogue pathologists were carrying the torch. The medicine supporting the claims was razor thin, at best. But it presented factual jury issues. How could silicone producers, implant makers, and their suppliers, possibly defend themselves in this litigation nightmare?

The litigation over silicone breast implants grew to become

the largest litigation morass in America. Over time, it simply overwhelmed the implant producers and other defendants. Ultimately, the largest implant producer, Dow Corning, an exemplar company, was forced into bankruptcy in 1998. Other well-known companies involved with either silicone or with the implants were also sued including General Electric, Bristol Myers Squibb, Dow Chemical, Union Carbide. Minnesota Mining & Manufacturing, and Foamex International, Inc. ("Foamex"). It was sued for a foam cover used on some of the implants. Smaller producers, like Bioplasty, were forced out of business.

For women seeking these preferred implants, there were no suppliers. This was a profound tragedy for women with breast cancer who desired implants. The silicone jell implant was as perfect as science could design. The surgery to implant it was straight forward. The silicone would ordinarily last for the life of the patient. Silicone was replaced with saline implants filled with salt water.

Over the years, there were a number of jury trials. In the beginning, the plaintiffs were winning with some million-dollar verdicts. The claims were supported by junk science, not sound medical opinions. Juries could not understand the complexities of the medical science; they sided with the testifying doctor they liked best and the woman who appeared to be injured. But then the tide turned. In the end, defendants won an estimated 80 percent of the lawsuits because all the medical studies and opinions supported them. But defending the mass of lawsuits were time consuming and expensive.

As the lawsuits and claims expanded exponentially, the ability to defend them all was compromised. Dow Corning's bankruptcy produced a $3.2 billion settlement fund. Out of necessity, it was joined by most of the other defendants. The total Global Settlement approached $4 billion. It was later distributed through a complex medical grid to approximately 200,000 women claiming some manner of illness. The plaintiff's lawyers received excessively handsome fees for producing such a large fund. Only General Electric and Foamex refused to join in the settlement.

Throughout the 15-year history of these lawsuits, three Blue Ribbon Medical Panels sponsored by the FDA, the federal court and the manufacturers failed to find the presence of any disease caused by silicone implants. The United Kingdom, France, Germany, Australia, Spain and the European Union all examined the science and found no reason to support any alleged disease claim. Silicone implants continued to be sold and used all over the world, except in the United States. Eventually, the FDA, which had suspended their approval during the litigation, lifted the suspension. Today, the same silicone implants from the 1980s and 1990s are currently products of choice by plastic surgeons, with slight improvements to the covers to reduce ruptures. They continue to provide exceptional relief to women seeking breast replacement or enhancement. In essence, almost $4 billion was paid to settle litigation that was baseless.

Foamex was one of the manufacturers sued in this massive litigation. It manufactured the polyurethane foam selected from an intermediary by Bristol Myers Squibb. Without its knowledge, the foam was being used as implant covers in order to provide a soft surface to avoid capsular contractions by the implant. The medical theory for this was that the scar tissue from the surgery would interface with the porous, soft foam cover glued to the implant rather than hardening against the implant's silicone cover. Capsular contraction of the scar tissue against the silicone covered implant was a vexing problem for a small percentage of women after surgery. This would cause the implant to deform, creating a need for more surgery.

We defended Foamex. Our defense in this case lasted five years before we obtained a summary judgement dismissing all the federal claims. Over time, the state courts also adopted the dismissal. The lawsuits we were forced to successfully defend were baseless on at least two counts. First, Foamex did not participate in the decision to use foam as a cover. It sold its bulk foam in blocks larger than mattresses to an intermediary foam distributor company located in Chicago. That company cut the foam into thin, Kleenex like sheets to be used in hospitals as absorbent wipes; it then sold the foam sheets to Bristol Myers. Second, the claim against the silicone implant was itself bogus. The defense cost Foamex a total of $13 million dollars. Under the American Rule, after dismissal, Foamex was not reimbursed for its attorneys' fees.

What was so wrong with the American legal system that it nearly destroyed a valuable and blameless medical product and its principal manufacturer? To answer that question, we must look at the medical history of silicone breast implants.[44]

There were two parallel courses relative to silicone breast implants and the 400,000 women who had them. One track was all of the litigation mostly centered in the federal court in Birmingham, Alabama. Judge Sam Poynter was diligently trying to manage all of the lawsuits, expanding claim numbers, and the hysteria they were causing.

The other track was centered in the medical community and, by inference, the FDA that had suspended the acceptance of the implants as approved medical devices in 1991. This track was a search for the truth to allay the concerns for all of the women and to return a valuable product for use in future breast cancer treatment.

An excellent, albeit brief, summary of these two tracks was published by Kristen E. Schleiter, JD, LLM in the *AMA Journal of Ethics,* "Illuminating the Art of Medicine." The article reports that in 1994, the same year that the Dow Corning settlement of $3.2 billion was approved, the largest settlement in class action history, the medical community was

---

[44] *See* Mai Brooks, History of Breast Silicone Implant Litigation 1977-1999 (January 13, 2009). Retrieved from http://ezinearticles.com/?History-of-Breast-Silicone-Implant-Litigation—1977-1999&id=1877909

reporting on the safety of silicone implants:

> *In June of 1994, the* New England Journal of Medicine *published a study by Mayo Clinic epidemiologists that found no increased risk of connective tissue disease in women with silicone gel breast implants. In 1995, the Journal followed with yet another study – this one larger and more refined – that found no association between implants and connective tissue disorders. As a result of the studies, the American College of Rheumatology issued a statement in 1995 asserting that the evidence was "compelling" that "silicone implants expose patients to no demonstrable risk for connective-tissue or rheumatic disease", and that "anecdotal evidence should no longer be used to support this relationship in the courts or by the FDA." In 1997, the American Academy of Neurology reviewed existing silicone gel breast implant studies and concluded that there was no link between the implants and neurological disorders. In the same year,* the Journal of National Cancer Institute *published a review of studies and concluded that breast implants did not cause breast cancer.*

These medical conclusions received further support over the next five years. The independent medical panel Judge Poynter appointed to assist the court, which cost $800,000, concluded that the implants did not cause disease. Following that report, the Institute of Medicine published its 400-page report that silicone implants do not cause autoimmune disease. Finally, in 2006, fifteen years after the FDA created the ban, the FDA removed the ban. Silicone breast implants returned to the market.

For 15 years, litigation with no proven accepted medical basis harmed women in the U.S seeking implants. It removed the silicone implant from their medical treatment, unless they sought treatment in another country. For 15 years, this medically baseless litigation caused unnecessary medical treatment for thousands upon thousands of women. For 15 years, many women with silicone implants lived with the fear that their implants might cause them a disease in the future. For 15 years, companies that had provided a safe and coveted cancer treatment for women were forced into defending litigation with no proven medical basis. Billions of dollars were spent by them to buy their peace. Even worthy companies had to declare bankruptcy.

When we look back at the Silicone Breast Implant Litigation, what does it tell us? What lessons, if any, can we learn?

It is redundant to compare what happened in the United States to the same situation in England. We already know the result. The silicone breast implant was not only the source of no litigation in England but also remained available.

The mistakes in the U.S. justice system are graphically on display. The litigation never would have started but for lay-juries being fooled into buying into junk medical science. They had no education or other basis to know better. Then it exploded from there. No judge was able to intervene.

Perhaps the real winners were all the plaintiff's lawyers who received a lot of money for filing lawsuits and handling this massive and unnecessary litigation. It was likely to be hundreds of millions of dollars. This was really good work to be had. A large number of defense attorneys also received millions of dollars for defending the litigation. The $13 million it cost to successfully defend Foamex was paid by its insurance policies.

Another conclusion was voiced by Ms. Schleiter in her AMA article. *See, Supra.* It invited us to place part of the blame on the shameless doctors who created, and then promoted, the litigation:

The silicone breast implant litigation of the nineties is

> *notable for (the) way in which judges and juries overlooked an astonishing lack of scientific evidence, while plaintiffs and their attorneys raked in millions. The hysteria and hype that the lawsuits generated caused some medical device companies to bankrupt or leave the implant market altogether. More recently, doctors' roles in asbestos litigation have prompted the U.S. Chamber of Commerce to call for an investigation into their conduct (and that of lawyers) in the "explosion of meritless and abusive asbestos claims.". While physicians have affirmative duty to assist in the administration of justice, those who are involved in litigation must testify honestly, without the influence of financial compensation, and with the interests of patients in mind.*

How could this happen? Only in America...a nation of lawyers.

LEAD IN PAINT (1997-2009)

The use of lead in paint was instrumental to the improvement of living conditions in the U.S. beginning in the 1920s. It prevailed for decades and was vital during World War II. But alas, "no good deed goes unpunished." Its reward was to become a Mass Tort.

Lead is a soft, dense, heavy metallic element found in nature, usually by surface mining. It's commonly used today in lead-acid batteries, weights, solders, pewters, fusible alloys, bullets and x-ray shields.[45] It is also used in specialty paints, which share a history of lead in paint used for decades in the early twentieth century.

Lead has been around and used in a variety of ways for much of the history of mankind. It was one of the earliest metals discovered, with estimates beginning in 7000 B.C. in Egypt and 3000 B.C. in Rome.[46] It was widely used in Rome for water pipes. Lead dishes were common in Rome as were lead-based cosmetics. Lead coins have been discovered in China that date to 4000 B.C. During the Dark Ages, it was widely used for not only many forms of plumbing and water management but also roofing, statues and church windows. The windows of glass and lead can last forever. Because lead has a sugary taste it was added to wine and food recipes in

---

[45] *See* Protect your Family from Exposures to Lead, United States Environmental Protection Agency. Retrieved from https://www.epa.gov/lead/protect-your-family-exposures-lead.

[46] History of Lead Us, IDC Technologies. Retrieved from http://www.idc-online.com/technical_references/pdfs/chemical_engineering/History_of_Lead_Use.pdf

France as a sweetener.[47]

At the turn of the twentieth century, white lead in paint became the product of choice.[48] This new mixed paint product was embraced. Professional painters would mix white lead pigment into their paints and paint away. Everyone wanted it. First and foremost, leaded paint had a long useful life of decades compared to other existing paints at the time. It remained bright and clean for its life. In addition, lead paint could be washed without any deterioration. This was a godsend to hospitals because hospitals were an unsafe place to be a patient. They are full of sick people. But before lead paint, a hospital's walls and floors could not be safely washed or disinfected. The paint would wash off. The patient had the acute risk of catching whatever disease had been treated in the room prior to his arrival. Lead paint dramatically changed much of that — the walls and floors could now be washed. Hospital rooms could be disinfected. By 1922, lead paint had reached its peak; it was everywhere. It was endorsed — and often mandated with consumer laws — by both state and local governments in the United States. It was also being used in every country in the world, including England.

In the 1940s, the use of lead paint declined. The Glidden Company invented latex paint. It had many of the advantages of lead paint but did not require a painter to mix it. It was also cheaper. Ordinary folks could now buy paint in a can and paint for themselves. In addition, lead supplies for white lead in public paint were disappearing. The U.S. government commandeered most of the lead supplies during World War II to manufacture lead in ammunition. Lead paint was also demanded by the U.S. Navy to paint its war ships because it did not burn. Lead is credited with saving the lives of

---

[47] A Brief History of Lead, Clear Corps Detroit. Retrieved from http://clearcorpsdetroit.org/lead-faq/a-history-of-lead/

[48] The History of Lead Paint in the U.S., Arizona Hydro Pro. Retrieved from https://azhydropro.com/history-lead-paint-u-s/

thousands of seamen whose ships were set afire in naval combat or by torpedoes. After the war, white lead was still used in specialty paints applied by professional painters, but it was no longer the paint product of choice.

For much of its history, there were suspicions that lead caused diseases. The Romans suspected it may cause gout, but as we know today, gout has other causes. People still suffer gout despite leaded paint being out of use for decades. These beliefs persisted over the centuries, but medical science could not identify or pin down any specific disease. People coveted the advantages that lead products provided to their lives.

After World War II, medical studies were published blaming developmental illnesses in small children on lead exposure. Much of the housing built in the heyday of lead paint decades before was deteriorating. When lead paint finally begins to fail, lead dust and chips fall on the floor. They taste like sugar. Small children, crawling on the floor and putting most of the things they found directly into their mouths, were swallowing all the lead dust they could find. Lead poisoning has a permanent effect on the brains of children. It decreases their mental capability. In severe cases, children would become developmentally stunted.

As a result of these discoveries, in the 1950s some cities banned lead paints. The paint industry voluntarily prohibited the use of lead paint as an interior paint. By 1971, the federal Lead Poisoning Prevention Act was passed, followed in 1978 by a U.S. ban on consumer use of lead paint. Other restrictions were passed later. This left open what to do to remedy the potential for lead poisoning in children in the old housing stock in the U.S.

Simple remediation was available to homeowners of old houses. They could clean their floors removing any lead dust. They could watch and supervise their infant children, so they would not be exposed by eating things on the floor. They could repaint the walls, covering the existing lead paint. They could remove the lead paint — an expensive process — and replace it with new paint or paneling. They could monitor the health of their children to assure no lead poisoning was occurring by testing them seasonally.

While all of these methods were available, further studies showed a troubling trend. Children were being poisoned in low-income areas. The numbers were larger than anticipated. At one point in the 1990s, a report opined that as many as three million children were poisoned. Further, millions of old houses required remediation and the cost to do so exceeded $200 billion. The U.S. government did not have the stomach to accept and pay for it. How to accomplish this and who would pay for it? With three million potential child plaintiffs, what was needed were some lawyers with a class action lawsuit. After all, America has lawyers and that is the American way.

The product liability lawsuits being filed appeared to be doomed from the start. The lead paint had been sold and applied many decades before, so there were no records of whose paint was in anyone's house. There was no one to identify and sue. Chemical analysis by mass spectrometry could not identify any specific company's paint product. All the formulas had the same white lead. Many of the paint companies had gone out of business or had changed ownership. Additionally, the lead paint they sold was not only thought to be a safe product of choice for homes, hospitals and the U.S. Navy, but also it was approved and mandated by every government.

No one had any reason to believe the paint was a hazard. At that time, while a few medical papers opined that lead in paint might be a problem, other papers, including one from Harvard Medical School, found the opposite to be true. In the 1950s the paint industry stepped forward to voluntarily prohibit the use of lead paint in housing. This was at a time when the U.S. government was still approving the use of lead paint. In essence, there was no one to sue because the product had been considered safe by everyone. The fact that over the decades the lead paint wore out and deteriorated did not mean that it was a defective product when sold many years before. Over time, everything wears out. If you do not replace old, worn out tires, they will cause automobile accidents. So it is with leaded paint. Moreover, the paint companies acted responsibly, more so than the U.S. government.

The plaintiffs' attorneys pursuing lead poisoning claims for children faced a host of defenses to their traditional lawsuits for negligence or product liability. In the end, their efforts failed, and those cases were dismissed.

Having thus far failed, the lawyers seized on a novel new theory, "public nuisance." They alleged that the paint companies had created a public nuisance by selling lead paint that was deteriorating today, and thus had to bear the "cost of cleaning it up." On its face the claim was problematic. This was a product liability claim that had no merit. How can it morph into a "public nuisance" lawsuit? Nevertheless, lawsuits were filed in seven state courts. It found traction in both Rhode Island and California. The suits languished in the other states.

A few of today's paint companies are long-standing. Sherwin Williams and Glidden are two of them. They existed in the 1900s when white lead pigment was used. As a result, they were sued in the Lead in Paint Litigation.

Glidden is owned by ICI PLC, the same London based large chemical company with the ammonia nitrate business. When the lawsuits began, ICI PLC called me. I met with Nigel Payton, the ICI Paint's general counsel, at Glidden headquarters in Cleveland. Not much was known about Glidden's long-ago history when lead was used in paint. Deep research and document review revealed that Glidden's old white lead business was one of several old companies Glidden had acquired. They were separate, independent companies but owned by Glidden as a parent. In the 1950s, Glidden had sold these companies, including the white lead one, to Millennium Chemical Company. It was listed on the New York Stock

Exchange. We took the view that Millennium owed Glidden the defense for the use of white lead pigment years before because it had acquired and now owned that company. While this was not well received, Millennium did undertake the defense of the Rhode Island lead paint litigation.

We monitored the lead lawsuits until they were all dismissed. We never had to defend or try a single case. All of that fell on Millennium's shoulders. When the lawsuits were finally closed, Millennium sued ICI, PLC in New York City to recover all of the monies, including attorneys' fees, it had paid for the defense. ICI, PLC retained the Debevoise law firm to defend it. Millennium lost that trial. Millennium appealed the case and lost again. The Lead in Paint Litigation ended well for ICI, PLC and Glidden, not so well for Millennium.

The Lead Paint Litigation does not present the host of abuses normally encountered in a Mass Tort, but it is still of interest in addressing the problems with litigation in America.

On the one hand, the lead paint producers did nothing wrong. When the leaded paint was invented, it was embraced by everyone, including all governments in the U.S. and around the world. But, alas, over a long time, decades, it was discovered that the wonder product used in old housing could finally begin to deteriorate. It could become a hazard for young children if simple, available steps are not taken to manage or avoid their exposure.

On the other hand, the U.S. is left with perhaps three million children suffering deficit disorders in old worn-out houses. More may be on the way. The old housing stock remains with old lead paint. The obvious question is where is the U.S. government in addressing this problem and abating it going forward?

WORLD TRADE CENTER (2001)

Most of us remember where we were on September 11, 2001, when the World Trade Center collapsed. It was a horrific mass disaster, surpassing Oklahoma City. It took years to find and punish Osama Ben Laden. Of course, in a Nation of Lawyers you can expect a huge Mass Tort lawsuit to be filed in New York City.

On September 11, 2001, Osama Bin Laden directed two commercial passenger planes, loaded with 91,000 litres of flammable jet fuel, to crash into each of the World Trade Center Twin Towers in New York City. The crashes succeeded in collapsing both towers, killing 2,753 innocent occupants on that fateful morning.

The collapses caused damage and destruction to the adjoining buildings. Building No. 7 also collapsed because of the impacts. It was estimated that the pile of debris containing building contents, glass, steel and concrete was twenty-seven stories high. It consumed an area the size of many city blocks. Fires burned continuously.

The smoke and developing clouds of debris-laden dust which covered the site were blown across New York City like a snowstorm. Residents of New York City, near and far, who breathed the dust soon developed what was labelled "World Trade Center Cough."

More than 15,000 workers, firemen, policemen and responders arrived quickly to search for victims. Then they completed the immense task of removing the debris to Staten Island where it was processed. In all, it is estimated that 1,462,000 tons of debris were removed and then sifted through over an eight-month period; it included 4,257 body parts.

In addition to first responders, immediately after the

Towers fell, additional volunteers and resources were requested to help first with the search and rescue and then with the debris removal. Four of the volunteers were large construction companies headquartered in New York City.

Turner Construction Company ("Turner") is a worldwide family-owned construction business in New York City. Its revenue in 2000 exceeded ten billion dollars. Turner constructed many well-known buildings including Madison Square Garden and the Whitney Museum of American Art, as well as tall towers in Malaysia, Mexico and Indonesia. Turner marshalled some its substantial resources of equipment and manpower. Within hours they were voluntarily dispatched to the site where they were put to work for months.

The control of the site was politically confusing. It was "under the control" of the City of New York and State of New York, the EPA, FEMA, OSHA, and the FBI. Everyone tried to be in charge. The head of the EPA, Christine Todd Whitman, promptly declared that the debris site was "safe" without ever having undertaken competent air sampling or testing. President George W. Bush came to the scene. He officially supported the opinion of the EPA, reassuring the workmen and all of New York City.

One thing should have been apparent from the beginning. The dust and smoke from the debris was going to be toxic, a "witch's brew," although it was not known *how* toxic. The buildings, built in the 1960s, were filled with tons of asbestos interior wall coverings, which were banned decades ago. Building No. 7 contained, in its subterranean vaults, the electrical transformers for parts of the city. Although it was not revealed until much later, as much a 103,000 pounds of polychlorinated biphenyl (PCB, a banned carcinogen) were released when the old transformers were crushed. Years ago, PCBs were widely used as coolant fluids for electrical equipment. They were now burned into the smoke. Moreover, all the offices in the buildings were loaded with electrical equipment that was destroyed; it released a host of toxic chemicals when the buildings collapsed. This toxic stew was mixed into the ever-present concrete dust released by the debris in the search and removal activity. The toxic smoke was present for 99 days.

After eight months, the site was cleared, but by then workers were developing respiratory problems, persistent coughs, and diseases. A litany of respiratory diseases was related to this cough — some were fatal — with many causing disabilities. It is estimated that the dust has caused 70 kinds of cancer. As a result, the lawsuits on behalf of the workers began. To say that New York City is litigious is an understatement. In all, more than 10,000 workers sued; they claimed injuries with potential claims worth billions of dollars because of their large numbers. It is presently estimated that as many as 400,000 people in the city have been affected by the debris dust.[49]

Turner, the volunteer and Good Samaritan who rushed men and equipment to the scene, was dragged into defending these massive lawsuits. Remember, "No good deed goes unpunished."

In the World Trade Center ("WTC") lawsuits to recover monies for the diseases of first responders and site workers from debris dust, my role was a consultant, not a trial defense attorney. Because of this limited role, my memory concerning dates is fuzzy. It was fifteen years ago. I received a telephone call from Turner's management in, I believe, 2003. The next day I went into their tall building lobby in New York City to attend a litigation defense conference.

Present in the Turner conference room were six men and one woman. The men were executives and construction

---

[49] Caroline Bankoff, What We Know About How 9/11 Has Affected New Yorkers' Health, 15 Years Later, New York Intelligencer (September 10, 2016). Retrieved from http://nymag.com/intelligencer/2016/09/15-years-later-how-has-9-11-affected-new-yorkers-health.html.

managers of Turner; the woman was the General Counsel. Turner had just been sued in the worker's lawsuits. They were in disbelief that this was happening. Further, members of the press were in their lobby, seeking Turner's response.

Turner was discussing how to involve its insurance company, determining who in the company would manage the litigation defense, who would interview lawyers to defend it, how to repair its public image from potential bad press, including responding to the press downstairs. The General Counsel was not the dominant speaker; she stared at me and wondered why I was there at all. Since I was there, I tried to make myself useful. I decided to prepare a press release for Turner to present to the press waiting downstairs. When we did jury research in the Supper Club case, we learned that you can only have three themes. After three, jurors tune out. I have kept that advice close for all these years. So, I created three themes for Turner's press release.

When I arrived at Turner, I waited in their lobby for nearly an hour while the meeting was convening. A coffee table book about Turner, with many pictures of the impressive buildings it had constructed in New York City, was on the table. I read through it. Turner had, indeed, an impressive history of construction. This was my opening paragraph in the press release: Turner has a long and respected history in New York. It is a valuable and honorable citizen, citing a few examples.

Second, immediately following the WTC collapse, Turner made the decision to help in any way it could. It marshalled resources, sent them to the scene and was involved in finding survivors and then cleaning up the debris. It did this as a volunteer without any expectation of a profit. It deserves to be praised, not sued.

Third, there is no legal reason to sue Turner at all. It was not in charge of the disaster site; it did not supervise the cleanup effort; it provided its employees with dust masks. There is no legal basis for these lawsuits. It was a Good Samaritan. Turner has served the City of New York well.

At the meeting, they finally moved to what to do about the press waiting downstairs. This is always a difficult problem for a company like Turner (recall the Humana discussion). There were widely differing opinions. I finally interrupted them to read my quickly written press release. There was silence as I read it. The General Counsel spoke first. She seemed surprised. She said, "Damn, that is good!" I was now a member of the team, helping Turner design all aspects of its defense. At my prompting, it included combining Turner with the other three sued construction companies for a unified, common defense effort. Turner and the other three companies adopted it, but each retained a separate law firm. Turner had an excellent New York law firm and attorney to defend it in the New York court.

Turner had convincing defenses to assert. New York has a statute that makes a contractor responsible for the safety of the workers at the work site. The statute assumes that the contractor is "in control" of the site. Turner was not in control of the WTC site or the pile of debris to be removed. It was taking its orders from others who were managing the site. The statute could not be used against Turner.

New York also had a "Good Samaritan" statute. When you respond to an accident scene to offer aid or assistance, the standard of care required is lessened by the circumstances at the accident. Turner was a "Good Samaritan." The WTC was a unique site. There had never before been anything like it. Thus, Turner's conduct of care was measured by the enormously difficult demands and circumstances at the site. Its conduct exceeded that standard. Moreover, Turner's employees had dust masks available to wear when working in the debris. Turner was not responsible for any other workers or first responders.

There was no allegation that Turner did anything wrong or improper in removing the debris. The claim was that the dust was toxic and poisoned the workers, so they should have been protected, but Turner had no knowledge of how toxic.

That information was monitored and controlled by the governmental entities overseeing the entire WTC collapse event, especially the Environmental Protection Agency.

With these defenses asserted, I attended the first Pre-Trial Conference for the combined cases. The conference room was overflowing with plaintiff and defense attorneys. The judge was looking to form steering committees to address a case management and scheduling order. It was obvious this would be a difficult litigation to manage because of its magnitude. Everything following the WTC collapse in New York was both outsized and difficult. But one thing was apparent. This was going to be an expensive lawsuit to defend; it could be staggering.

Shortly after the conference, my role was completed. I returned to Louisville and lost contact with the proceeding as it struggled forward. I learned later the court implemented a settlement conference procedure for all the workers lawsuits. The judge would coerce settlements. This would follow the MGM Grand Litigation management experience. Over time, it accomplished the task. The cost of defense was high, so large settlements were in order without regard to the valid defenses. The settlement pot was large, but more money came from Congress, WTC insurance (after more lawsuits) and other sources. The task of paying the proceeds to the claimants was also complicated and lengthy. Finally, years later, most aspects of the WTC tragedy aftermath were resolved. A new WTC building and memorial now stand where the debris had been.

There are two reasons to report on the WTC tragedy and resulting debris removal lawsuits. The event was the worst terrorist-caused disaster in American history. Correctly, Congress did not stick its head in the sand as before, but instead sent billions of dollars of relief. The U.S. responded to a tragedy in a meaningful way. But those funds went to victims — not the workers. They had to resort to lawsuits.

The fault for the workers injuries from the debris dust lay with the U.S. government and the City of New York, not the contractors. The EPA took responsibility for the site, then falsely reported the toxicity of the atmosphere. So did the U.S. President, George W. Bush. The U.S. government should have compensated the injured workers for its mistakes. It did not.

That said, of this I remain sure: A lot of lawyers made a whole lot of money.

JUDGES: SELECTED BY POLITICS

When we look at the unseemly explosion of litigation in the United States, we must also lay blame on the judges. To prevent any seemingly kingly authority, the Founding Fathers created Article II, Section 2 of the U.S. Constitution which gives the *President* (as an elected official) *the power to appoint all federal judges.*[50] As a further constraint on any kingly authority, the appointment requires confirmation by the citizen-elected U.S. Senate.[51] This aversion to kingly authority planted the seeds for all federal judges to be selected forevermore by politicians. Today, politicians now play a dominating role in the U.S. judiciary, both federally and at the state level.

The original intention of the appointment process for federal judges served as a check and balance on the executive branch. Its purpose was to protect the judiciary from being subject to popular opinion, so they could make decisions based on impartial interpretations of the law instead of what decision would get them re-elected.[52] These safeguards were instituted under a noble premise, but the current political climate indicates that the process is not working as it was intended.

Experience and qualifications are not necessary prerequisites for federal judicial appointment. Unfortunately, today political party affiliation dictates who will become a

---

[50] U.S. Const. art. II, § 2, cl. 2.

[51] *See* Christopher L. Eisgruber, *Politics and Personalities in the Federal Appointments Process*, 10 Wm. & Mary Bill Rights J. 177, 180 (2001).

[52] *See* Dmitry Bam, *Tailored Judicial Selection*, 39 UALR L. REV. 521, 522 (2017).

federal judge, as opposed to their legal expertise.[53] Moreover, once appointed, all federal judges serve for life.[54] Each judge self-determines whether he is still able to perform his duties at a high standard.

Separate from the federal court system is the state court system, which is governed by state laws. These systems vary state by state. As a member of both the Kentucky and Florida bar associations, I can show you two examples of state judge selection. In Kentucky, judges in all of the levels of court — Circuit Court, Court of Appeals, and Supreme Court — are elected for six years.[55] State election laws prohibit judicial candidates from running on a political party ticket.[56] In contrast, Florida's judicial selection process is more of a hybrid system.[57] Each of the judges for the Appeals Court is chosen by a Judge's Committee and then recommended to the governor for appointment.[58] After one year, they stand for a bipartisan election with a yes or no vote. The circuit court

---

[53] See James L. Huffman, Politics and Judicial Independence: A Proposal for Reform of Judicial Selection in Oregon, 39 Willamette L. Rev. 1425, 1429 (2003).

[54] *FAQs: Federal Judges*, U.S. Courts, https://www.uscourts.gov/faqs-federal-judges (last visited Mar. 14, 2019).

[55] *See* Ryan Fortson & Kristin S. Knudsen, A Survey of Studies on Judicial Selection, 32 Alaska Justice Forum 1, 8 (2015).

[56] *See* Ryan Fortson & Kristin S. Knudsen, A Survey of Studies on Judicial Selection, 32 Alaska Justice Forum 1, 8 (2015), https://www.uaa.alaska.edu/academics/college-of-health/departments/justice-center/alaska-justice-forum/32/2-3summerfall2015/_documents/atab1.pdf.

[57] *Judicial Selection in the States: Florida*, NATIONAL CENTER FOR STATE COURTS, http://www.judicialselection.us/judicial_selection/index.cfm?state=FL (last visited Mar. 15, 2019).

[58] *id.*

judges are elected directly with a term of six years.[59]

Like Kentucky and Florida, many states select their judges through a popular election where their skill, experience or qualifications are not well known to the voting public.[60] The ability to run a successful judicial campaign is often driven by name recognition or prior political experience.[61] The most qualified candidate is not always the one running for judge; it may be the one who can raise the most money.[62] By and large, the trial lawyers know who the better judges will be. But their role in the selection process is small, if at all.

The increasing politicization of appointing Federal judges is now dominating the news. This has been recently highlighted in the selection of Supreme Court justices. Each party wants a judge who will be supportive of its agenda. So, the party in power rules the day. One of the worst examples is the recent appointment of a host of federal judges by Republicans Senator Mitch McConnell and President Donald Trump. They tried their best to pack the courts. Because their appointed judges are so strongly party affiliated, we can expect that some number will be biased and/or unqualified. This manipulation harms our civil justice system.

The departure from the English system is dramatically apparent. In Britain, the selection of judges has been a straightforward and long-standing process beginning at the

---

[59] *id.*

[60] *See* Ryan Fortson & Kristin S. Knudsen, A Survey of Studies on Judicial Selection, 32 Alaska Justice Forum 1, 8 (2015), https://www.uaa.alaska.edu/academics/college-of-health/departments/justice-center/alaska-justice-forum/32/2-3summerfall2015/_documents/atab1.pdf.

[61] *See* Andrew Cohen, *An Elected Judge Speaks Out Against Judicial Elections*, The Atlantic (Sept. 3, 2013), https://www.theatlantic.com/national/archive/2013/09/an-elected-judge-speaks-out-against-judicial-elections/279263/.

[62] *id.*

time of the Magna Carta, when deciding legal disputes were taken away from the King in favor of a legal system of courts. It has survived and been enhanced over hundreds of years. The process starts with a Judge's Commission seeking the best candidates among the independent barristers. Barristers are the trial lawyers for British courts. Barristers seeking judicial appointment can apply to the Judge's Commission; the Commission members may also solicit selected Barristers. The Commission selects three candidates as finalists.

In order to become a Barrister, after receiving a law degree the prospect must be accepted at the Inns of Court (a professional association for Barristers of England and Wales). He must then pass a Bar Professional Training Court exam. If he passes, he goes on to complete a one-year apprenticeship. Then he can practice as a trial lawyer. Only about one in ten Barristers are selected to become Queen's Counsel. They are often considered to be legal scholars. Queen's Counsel are usually selected by the Judge's Commission. The three finalists are carefully reviewed for the position as Judge. The "winner" is presented to the King or Queen for appointment as a Judge. He must retire by age 70; he does not serve for life as in the U.S. It is a high honor to be selected as a judge in England.

This English process is superior in many respects to the American approach. The British judges are already legal scholars and thus knowledgeable; they serve as protectors of British common law. They are the best of the best, gaining expertise by being first Barristers and then Queen's Counsel. The selection by the Judge's Commission is in essence a selection by their peers. *This is vital to a healthy judicial system.*[63] When the Barristers practice cases before a newly appointed judge, they want a person of excellence. If they choose an inept and unknowledgeable candidate, they must

---

[63] *See* generally Mary L. Volcansek, Judicial Selection: Looking at How Other Nations Name Their Judges, 53 *The Advoc.* (Texas) 95, 96 (2010).

try their cases before an inferior judge. The final decision on the appointment of a Judge is made by the King or Queen, who is not elected.[64] Thus, politics play no role in the judicial selections in Great Britain.[65]

In England, the judges are tenured, and their independence is assured. They may not be sued for carrying out their judicial functions. Neither the government nor Parliament may publicly discuss matters pending in court. In English civil cases, the judge's role is to decide the entire case. *The judges decide the legal issues, the findings of facts and then the amount to award in damages.*

As you can see, there are major constraints on filing civil lawsuits in England. As a result, there are fewer judges there than in the U.S. Their small numbers are esteemed, indeed. In the U.S., political judges can be seen everywhere, in great numbers. It is estimated there are 30,000 state court judges and 1,700 Federal judges. Besides being a nation of lawyers, we are also a nation of judges.

---

[64] *Id.*

[65] *Id.*

THE STATION NIGHTCLUB (2003)

Here is another example of the problem with our federal judges, who are appointed for life. The fire in The Station Club in Rhode Island mirrors the lawsuits from the other large fire disasters.

On a cold February night in 2003, in West Warwick, Rhode Island, a crowd was gathering at The Station nightclub. The popular band Great White was playing that evening. As the band prepared to play, 462 people crowded into the nightclub. Many had been drinking; they believed they were in for a festive night. Television station WPRI-TV sent a cameraman to record the show. A radio DJ was also present for the dancing to take place following the band's performance. When the band set up on the stage in the alcove that afternoon, they brought with them their three gerds. Gerds are pyrotechnic devices that spray electric sparks up to fifteen feet for about fifteen seconds. The band used the gerds often for their performances. They are an exciting fireworks-type of display that excites the crowd when the show begins.

They started playing Great White's most popular song, the 1991 *Billboard* hit "Desert Moon." The crowd responded enthusiastically. This was "game on" in West Warwick. As the lights went down, the band's manager set off the gerds, spraying the electrical sparks away from the band. The spray of sparks splattered the walls and ceiling around the band. The show was spectacular.

Then the sparks began to ignite the black non-acoustic foam that had been glued to the walls and ceiling for soundproofing. In prior years, the neighbors had complained about the loud noise from the nightclub. The tenants, the Derderian brothers — who leased the building rather than owning it outright — purchased basic black, dimpled sheets of polyurethane packaging foam from a local distributor. They glued them to the walls and ceiling surrounding the stage in the alcove to deaden the noise. The foam they purchased was not acoustic foam fit for a nightclub. That foam would have met applicable fire codes because it would be fire and flame resistant... and it would also be expensive. It would cost twice as much. The Derderians purchased the cheaper polyurethane packaging foam sheets.

At The Station, a tragic event was occurring. Soon the walls and ceiling were smoldering and then aflame. At first, the 462 patrons assumed this was part of the show. But it was not. As the smoke started filling the nightclub, the fire spread across the surface of the foam sheets. The patrons began exiting the building. There were four exits, but most patrons headed toward the front doors where they had entered. Within minutes, the foam in the alcove had reached "flashover." All the foam on the walls and ceiling was burning at the same time, producing copious amounts of black smoke. By then, panic had overcome everyone clamoring for the exits.

The band barely escaped the fire through the west exit at the stage. But because the fire was engulfing the stage alcove, the west stage exit was closed off to the patrons by the fire. Another exit had been blocked by a large table to accommodate the overflow crowd. Escaping the fire was becoming more difficult.

The black acrid smoke was now filling the nightclub. A crush of patrons was moving to exit the front door and tumbling outside. Within five minutes, the nightclub was filled with the black, toxic smoke. The smoke overcame those still in the nightclub and obscured the other two smaller exit doors. The fire trucks arrived, and firemen began pulling people out the front doors. At the end of the tragic night, 100 people were dead, 230 were injured and only 132 escaped unscathed. The bodies around the front door were stacked in layers. Surprisingly, the firemen found live patrons lying under the dead ones. The ones below had been shielded from the fire by the bodies above them. The fire scene that morning was ghastly.

After the tragic event, fire safety authorities investigated the fire and conducted fire modelling. They had the unique benefit of the TV cameraman who had recorded the entire event, including the onset of the fire, until he also fled. They were in luck to have a real time video of the crowd, the start of the fire and its growth and spread as well as evidence of the panic of the patrons.

The investigation discovered an array of fire code and safety standard violations. The illegality of The Station was monstrous. Inexplicably, all of these serious violations had been overlooked or intentionally disregarded by the Rhode Island State Fire Marshall during his inspections. Two of these inspections occurred after the illegal foam was glued to the walls. The fire code and safety standard violations included:

1. The use of non-acoustic flammable foam on the walls of a public building violating a fire code.
2. The absence of sprinklers in the building. The original building built in 1946 as a restaurant was exempt. When it was converted to a nightclub, sprinklers became mandatory under the code but were never installed.
3. The building was over-crowded, exceeding its occupancy limit set by the code.
4. The exits were not properly marked, and the exit doors were not approved under the code.
5. The overcrowding caused furniture to be moved blocking one of the exits.
6. The band area for gerds was too small for their use under the code, which made them illegal. The band claimed the owners approved the gerds; the owners claimed the gerds were a surprise and never mentioned.

The conclusion of the fire safety agencies after fire modelling was that sprinklers would have suppressed the fire sufficiently to allow everyone to escape; acoustic flame-retardant foam would not have been ignited by the gerds electrical sparks; the gerds should not have been used at all in that space; over-crowding prevented patrons from escaping as did the exit blocked by furniture.

The Derderian brothers and the band manager were charged with 200 counts of involuntary manslaughter, two counts for each death for two different degrees of criminal manslaughter. The criminal trials never occurred because they bargained guilty pleas. Nevertheless, the band manager served four years in prison, with six years suspended. One brother, the active owner, served the same sentence as the band manager. The other less active brother received a ten-year suspended sentence. The Station nightclub was without either fire or workers compensation insurance (three fire victims were employees). The owners were fined more than one million dollars for all the violations.

An interesting aside is that the less active brother was a WPRI-TV reporter. He personally sent the TV cameraman to record the concert as part of a TV program he was doing on "nightclub safety." Moreover, a year earlier he had done a TV report on the flammability of polyurethane foam. On top of that, on a prior occasion a band had used gerds which had set the foam on the wall on fire. The fire was quickly put out with a fire extinguisher. The Station Club knew its foam wall covering was flammable and a fire hazard from the gerds! The similarities to the Supper Club, MGM Grand and San Juan fires years earlier are eerie but this one was more preventable.

The tragic event had a devastating impact in the small West Warwick community. It is a community of hard working, lower income Rhode Islanders. Many of them lacked the necessary medical insurance to cover their treatment for injuries. Many of the patrons that managed to escape suffer from post-traumatic stress disorder.

The Station had no insurance, no money and no assets. So, who will pay? How will the victims be compensated? Enter, stage left, the lawyers.

As a result of the San Juan fire litigation, which did not work as well for the plaintiff's lawyers, the usual suspects did not come to Rhode Island. The lawyers that worked Beverly Hills, MGM and San Juan stayed home. Rather, a well-known and respected lawyer in Providence, Mark Mandell, led the charge with other local lawyers. They searched far and wide to find possible defendants to sue for the massive personal injury claims suffered by The Station patrons. The obvious defendants were the Derderians and the band. But they had limited resources. They were "dead in the water." The fire investigation laid the fault for the tragic catastrophe at their feet. That fault was aided and abetted by the State Fire Marshall's cursory inspection of The Station. But the lawyers were creative. Anyone who had any contact with the event, or the building, was fair game to them. They filed extensive lawsuits. The cast of defendants who settled and their settlements, according to Wikipedia, included:

- The Tour Group and Derderians came up with less than $2 million. The Derderians took bankruptcy.

- The State of Rhode Island and Town of West Warwick were sued for the failed fire safety inspections by the Fire Marshall. They settled for $10 million.

- WPRI-TV paid $30 million on the basis of patrons' testimony that the TV cameraman took pictures and impeded escape efforts by patrons.

- Budweiser and its distributor offered $21 million. A Budweiser truck was in the parking lot partially blocking the egress of the fire trucks to the scene.

- The radio station and its parent company, who had promoted the show, paid $22 million.

- Home Depot and Polar Guard, an insulation company, paid $5 million for the foam product allegedly on the ceiling that burned in the fire and was traced to them.

- A company that produced foam in the band's speakers, which burned in the fire, contributed less than $1 million.

- Sealed Air Corporation agreed to pay $25 million for allegedly having manufactured polyurethane foam sold to The Station.

- American Foam Corporation paid $6.3 million as the local distributor who actually sold the polyurethane foam sheets to the Derderians.

- The Derdians were tenants, but the building owner, along with the pyrotechnic company and an alarm company, contributed $13.5 million.

- More than 90 defendants were sued in The Station Litigation so numerous smaller settlements were made, the last in 2008.

In all, $176 million was recovered for the victims. Many of the claims against the settling defendants listed above seem, at least to me, to be a stretch for finding any liability. But the "cost of defense" for a Mass Tort is high. Further, if there is even a scintilla of evidence or a hint of wrongdoing that can be found, the consequence in damages from a local jury trial could be large, indeed. The settlements bought their peace. They were glad — and relieved — to exit from the federal courthouse and the litigation.

Among the defendants was General Foam Corporation, who Mandell accused of making the polyurethane packaging foam that the Derderians eventually purchased. We took the defense of the litigation head on. We had been there before in the other cases, although not for this client and its insurance carrier, AIG. The defense seemed straight forward. This case could be won at trial just as we did in The Supper Club and San Juan.

All the lawsuits were consolidated in the Rhode Island U.S. District Court in Providence before Judge Ronald Lagueux. To me, he seemed a curious choice for such a large and complicated case. Judge Lagueux was seventy-three years old and took Senior Status two years earlier. Senior Status means the federal judge handles a reduced case load. He believed at the time he was not able to maintain a full schedule. He was correct because he was ill. I was told that he was being treated for cancer. As a result, this large case tended to languish in his court. It was often weeks before common motions would be decided and months between his in court pre-trial conference sessions. A judge who rules quickly and decisively, as Judge Bechtel did, is a trial lawyer's boon. Judge Lagueux was a trial lawyer's bane.

In the Station Fire Litigation, we had a clear shot at the same defense and procedure we employed before U.S. District Court Judge Russell in Oklahoma City to obtain an early dismissal. We pressed on with assimilating our defenses, which were numerous and persuasive. We would deal with Judge Lagueux's difficulties when the time came.

The parallels between the Oklahoma City case and The Station case were striking, except The Station case had additional dominating defenses, each one requiring a dismissal. As in Oklahoma, where Terry Nichols purchased a common product — fertilizer — for Timothy McVeigh's bomb from a Kansas farm store, the Derderians purchased common foam used in packaging from American Foam, a local distributor. They did not buy it directly from General Foam. McVeigh misused the fertilizer to make a bomb. The Derderians misused the foam to cover the walls and ceiling of the alcove for soundproofing. Using fertilizer for a bomb and common foam on nightclub walls are both illegal. Finally, in both cases the illegal conduct was more than negligence; it was criminal. The common law of one case in Oklahoma should apply to the common law of another case in Rhode Island, *stare decisis*. Moreover, the failure of the Fire Marshall was an additional defense.

I have defended a host of fire cases across the country for many products that allegedly caused a fire or burned in a fire, in addition to the Mass Torts recited in this book. Not one of those cases came even close to presenting all the intervening illegal acts and defenses of The Station and Fire Marshall for the disaster. Those intervening, superseding acts erase the plaintiffs' claims against General Foam, just as they did for ICI in Oklahoma City.

General Foam had yet another defense that, on its own, required its dismissal from the litigation. The foam used in The Station was purchased from the local American Foam Corporation in Providence. It is a large foam distributor. It purchased its big foam buns (each one larger than a mattress) from a number of foam producers across the country. The foam is relatively light in weight. It packs and ships easily across the U.S. American Foam had records of the purchases it made from those producers. But when American Foam cuts and processes the foam for different uses for resale, it does not trace the seller's foam from its inventory to the end products. Thus, the black foam packaging sheets it sold to the Derderians could not be traced back to any one of the selling foam producers through the records American Foam kept. Who manufactured the foam?

After the fire, left over remnants of the black foam sheets were found in the basement of The Station. This was the same black dimpled foam used for the walls. The plaintiff's lawyers got this foam. They sent it to a well-known testing laboratory in Illinois. By mass spectrometry the foam could be analyzed. Its density and chemical formulation could be determined with a high degree of accuracy. The lab performed the tests and reported the findings. Using discovery, we obtained the test results and took their depositions, verifying the accuracy. We also had the records of the large foam buns General Foam sold to American Foam for resale. We knew the precise density and chemical formulations. The tested foam from The Station did not match the General Foam product. The variances were significant. In point of fact, the black packaging foam sheets the Derderians purchased and glued to the walls of The Station were not manufactured by General Foam! The plaintiff's lawyers had proved this conclusive fact for us. This "alibi" defense was golden.

We were in a position to seek a dismissal of the lawsuit. But what about Judge Lagueux?

So, we prepared and filed a motion for a Federal Rule of Civil Procedure 56 Motion for Summary Judgement, just as we had done in Air Canada, Oklahoma City, Yonkers, and Silicone Implants, successfully. This is permitted when the facts are established, not disputed, and the law requires a dismissal. I discussed this with my partner, Sue Wettle. We had worked together for decades. She is an exceptional legal memoranda researcher and writer.

We anticipated that gaining a dismissal from Judge Lagueux might not be easy, so she did extensive legal research. She found a number of statutes and cases in Rhode Island that supported our legal arguments and mandated a dismissal. We also relied on the Oklahoma City case and opinions. *Stare decisis*. She drafted an exceptional legal Memorandum supporting our dismissal motion. In fact, when General Foam's General Counsel was flying to Rhode Island from

California for the oral argument, he read our papers. At breakfast the next day, he asked, "Who wrote the Memorandum?" I told him my partner, Sue Wettle. He said, "It is the best document I have ever seen."

Our legal Memorandum supporting the Summary Judgement Rule 56 Motion summarizes our arguments in the Introduction:

ARGUMENT

> Defendants General Foam Corporation, GFC Foam, LLC, PMC, Inc. and PMC Global, Inc. (collectively "GFC") move for summary judgement because the undisputed evidence shows the Plaintiffs cannot establish the essential elements of their claims for negligence, strict liability and breach of warranty, and GFC is entitled to judgement as a matter of law. First, Plaintiffs cannot establish by competent evidence that GFC manufactured the foam that was illegally installed at The Station nightclub. Second, even if they could identify the foam as GFC's product, there were alterations and modifications to GFC's packaging foam which substantially caused the injuries, thereby severing any potential for GFC's liability under R.I. Gen. Laws 9-1-32. Third, under the bulk supplier doctrine as adopted by the Rhode Island Supreme Court, GFC's explicit warnings about the packaging foams flammability to its customer American Foam discharged its duty as a bulk material product manufacturer. Fourth, GFC had no legal duty to prevent others from misusing its foam or to warn Plaintiffs about the danger presented by other's misuse. Moreover, numerous negligent and criminal acts, remote in time, place and character from GFC, intervened to cause Plaintiffs' injuries and broke any tenuous causal connection to GFC's sale of bulk foam

> to a knowledgeable downstream intermediary. Finally, there is no evidence of any express warranty or implied warranty of fitness for a particular purpose, nor any evidence of a breach of an implied warranty of merchantability concerning GFC's bulk foam.

Our confidence level was high for the oral argument. Frankly, given our defenses and Memorandum, I expected Judge Lagueux to drill Mark Mandell over why he should not dismiss the case. It would be shades of Judge Russell in Oklahoma City.

The oral argument atmosphere was disappointing, to say the least. Judge Lagueux was passive. I could not divine that he had even read our excellent Memorandum. The courtroom had the overpowering aroma of "home cooking." Could it be that there was not going to be any dismissals in Rhode Island? Judge Lageuex was going to take the lazy way out and not disappoint the dead and injured people of Rhode Island; justice will not be done. As I came to realize as I left the courtroom, our motion was going to be denied and it was.

Both General Foam and AIG now faced a new problem. It did not appear a dismissal of General Foam could be obtained in Rhode Island without a jury trial. The "cost of defense" just went up dramatically. Further, General Foam had an odd insurance policy with AIG. It required General Foam to pay all defense costs, including attorneys' fees, subject to being reimbursed when the litigation was closed. General Foam was paying for the defense, not AIG. This created an incentive for General Foam to settle the case and recover those costs. It did not pay the potential liability settlement sum; that was paid by AIG. AIG also had an incentive to obtain a settlement of the entire litigation, closing its books. It had seen more than enough of Rhode Island justice at our hearing. All of this came forward in a two-day conference at AIG in New York.

We opposed a settlement. We knew the case could, and eventually would, be won. The only question was when? But business decisions had to be made. They always rule the day. The case was settled for an amount we were not privy to, but it was for more than it should have been — probably by a lot. We had defended the litigation well. Some days you get the bear and some days the bear gets you.

The corruption of legal principles in America played out in The Station Litigation. The decision to not dismiss the lawsuit against General Foam, pure and simple, was a travesty of justice. If the English Rule applied, General Foam would have been dismissed early in the case and most certainly when the foam identification test results surfaced showing their foam was not used. Our litigation costs and attorneys' fees would have been running up for Mr. Mandell's clients to pay when General Foam finally won. He had accumulated the money in the settlement pot to pay them.

This begs the question of why was Judge Lagueux presiding over this case? In England, at age 72 and in ill health, he would have been retired. But in America he was appointed for life! Only he could decide not to continue; a choice he refused to make. Sad, indeed. Although Judge Legueux was an embarrassment, there were other U.S. District Court Judges in Rhode Island that were more capable for a case this large and important. The only conclusion I can draw is that the Rhode Island lawyers and their judge were determined to look after their own.

A comparison to England is obvious. In England the lawsuit would never have been filed against General Foam because:

(1) It did not sell the foam to the Derderians, American Foam did;

(2) General Foam notified American Foam that its common foam was flammable;

(3) The Derderians and American Foam chose to use the

common foam for an illegal purpose;

(4) gluing it to the walls and lighting the gerds were criminal acts;

(5) having done so, the Fire Marshall overlooked that illegal use;

(6) The Station nightclub was in violation of numerous fire codes;

(7) the band's use of gerds at all was illegal;

(8) the foam used in the building was not even made or sold by General Foam.

The English Rule would have protected General Foam.

Lastly, if the case were filed in England, the judge assigned to it would have dismissed it. Justice would have been served. End of story for the English comparison.

But this is the way it is with political judges appointed for life.

INSURANCE: DEFENSE COST SETTLEMENTS AND BAD FAITH CLAIMS

What role does insurance play in the conundrum of U.S. Tort litigation? As you have seen in my Mass Torts defenses, a big one! These companies have unwittingly funded, and thereby sustained, the problems in the U.S. civil Tort litigation system. This is particularly true when the insurance company decides to pay a cost of defense settlement to close out the litigation against the entity it has insured.[66]

Insurance is a business. The insurance companies make their profits by selling casualty or liability insurance, investing the proceeds wisely, and reducing the payments for claims as much as possible. According to a 2017 report by the casualty insurance industry, the ten largest U.S. companies wrote as much as $300 billion dollars in property and casualty insurance. As a consequence of this profit-making incentive, insurance companies often treat lawsuits against the insured individuals as risk and cost management.[67] They are skilled at it and employ a host of lawyers and actuaries to do it.

When an insured individual or entity commits a Tort, the insurance company is on the hook for two costs. The first is to pay for the liability caused by the insured's wrongful Tort.[68] If you rear end another vehicle, causing $25,000 in damage, your insurance company pays that amount to the other car's owner. If the other owner is also injured in the accident, it pays those damages as well.

If a lawsuit is filed against you, the insurer is responsible

---

[66] https://themissouritimes.com/56143/opinion-new-insurance-coalition-head-touts-more-tort-reform/.

[67] *Id.*

[68] *Id.*

for paying the costs of defending the lawsuit. It gets to pick the attorney to defend you because the company is paying the defense attorney. Because of this dual role, to some extent the insurer and its insured can become in conflict. The insured may want its conduct or product defended, believing it has done nothing wrong. His position is "defend me at all costs." This is not always in the insurance company's best interest. It wants to save money any way it can. If it can offer a settlement amount to resolve the claim for less than the risk of going through a jury trial plus the cost of the lawyers defending the insured, it will settle the case. It wants low cost and a profit, not a vindication of the insured.

Insurance companies can be their own worst enemies with cost of defense settlements. The larger the lawsuit and number of defendants, the larger the cost of defending it, as with my Mass Tort litigation. The cost of defending with lawyers becomes excessive for many of the peripheral defendants, and their insurers want to buy peace. Because the litigation is so large, and the consequential defense is so expensive, the insurer may pay a lot to settle. This often works against the other defendants and their insurers. As the plaintiff's lawyers gather more settlements, their settlement pot grows. This means they have more money to spend on the litigation. It is a vicious circle. Cost of defense settlements beget more cost of defense settlements. In the end, the insurance companies are the losers... until they sell new and more expensive insurance policies.

In 1869, the Supreme Court excluded insurance from the Commerce Clause of the U.S. Constitution. This meant that insurance companies would not be subject to federal regulation. As a result, insurance laws are enacted by each of the 50 states. All of the insurance regulations and cases of the 50 states are vast, often complex. Moreover, they are generally disadvantageous because the public is suspicious of and antagonistic toward insurance companies.

This massive body of law is beyond the scope of this book.

That said, however, there is one notable legal result, caused by lawsuits, that has evolved over the past sixty years. It has an impact on cost of defense settlements by insurers. This is commonly known as the doctrine of "Insurance Bad Faith." It requires insurance companies to act with "*utmost good faith.*" Thus, there is a magnifying glass for the conduct of insurers. As a result, litigation against them can be prevalent and often successful.

This "good faith" requirement opens the insurer to potential claims when performing its contractual duties. One is for an alleged breach of contract, *e.g.* it does not provide everything the contract could be construed to call for. The other is for the Tort of acting in bad faith. It is deemed careless in defending the insured. Consequential damages, those that are caused directly by bad conduct, can be assessed for either claim. The Tort claim can add on punitive damages if the conduct is deemed egregious. Thus, the insurance company acts at its own peril when making decisions affecting: (1) Its policy and limits, (2) The perceived realities about the claim, its defense and any potential settlement, and (3) The paramount interest of its insured.

As you can see, the complexities of insurance law and conduct by insurers creates a hazardous field for insurance companies. At least to some extent, this fuels their desire to pursue "cost of defense" settlements to end the claims and their exposure risk.

What is the "bad faith" insurance rule in England? The English courts do not permit consequential damages for alleged bad faith insurance claims. The test is the reasonableness of the decisions made by the insurer. Moreover, the English courts do not recognize a Tort claim for alleged bad faith arising from an insurance contract. There is no exposure or potential for punitive damages.

As with most things litigious in England, lawsuits are contained, not encouraged, and certainly not embellished. It should also be noted that insurance was invented in England in the seventeenth century to cover losses at sea. Insurance companies have been appreciated ever since.

ASBESTOS (1970 – ONGOING)

There is a Mass Tort where all the problems for insurers are magnified and on display. It is the largest and longest running Mass Tort litigation in U.S. history. It arises from the old industrial product, asbestos. It can be viewed as a waste of tens of billions of dollars which could have compensated the victims. This story is compelling, indeed.

Sometimes, just the sheer size of a problem makes it impossible to keep this nation of lawyers under control. In 2002, nearly 20 years ago, a study estimated that as much as $40 billion had been paid to lawyers in the asbestos litigation, rather than to the victims of the diseases caused by asbestos. The result is payments to law firms in the tens of billions of dollars — almost one and a half times more than the workers and their families receive. If there was a better way, tens of billions of dollars more could go to victims and their families. This demonstrates the worst of the civil litigation problem in the United States. Millions of words have been written about asbestos litigation from a host of different viewpoints. But they all agree on one thing. It is the biggest legal mess, ever. It continues to grow larger and messier each year. It may continue for more decades to come.

A 2002 study by the Rand Institute of Civil Justice[69] found that from the 1970s forward, there were 730,000 claims filed for asbestos related diseases. More than 6,000 companies had been sued. These claims have cost insurers and businesses over $70 billion. As a result of these claims, in 2002, it was estimated that the lawyers' fees and costs consumed 58 percent compared to the injured parties receiving 42 percent. Stated another way, the lawyers have received $40.6 billion dollars

---

[69] Rand Institute of Civil Justice, *Asbestos Litigation Costs and Compensation, An Interim Report*, 2002

in order to recover $29.4 billion dollars for the claimants. Think about these numbers. If the asbestos litigation were an ATM machine, in order to withdraw $100 that bank's fee will be $138, not $3. The litigation continues today, 18 years after this study was published. The total claims and costs today are staggering. It is estimated that between 12,000 and 15,000 people will die every year from asbestos exposure.

It is impossible to note and cover all of the asbestos issues in these pages. A book that is replete on this subject would be too heavy to carry. Nevertheless, asbestos and the resulting litigation graphically demonstrate what has gone so wrong with the U.S. civil justice system. It must be included, albeit superficially.

Asbestos has a signature disease only it causes, mesothelioma, a form of lung cancer. After years of exposure latency, it attacks lung tissue by hardening it. There is no cure! After just a few years from its onset, the lungs literally turn into cement. The victims try to breathe, gasping. Then take the last gasp and die. It is a painful and ugly death that no one should endure. It is devastating to the victims and their loved ones. I learned this when I participated in an asbestos trial in 2008.

The history of asbestos is long and complicated. For centuries it had been a miracle product. Asbestos is found in nature and can be easily extracted by mining. Once a vein is opened, it tends to become wide and deep, offering asbestos extraction for years. The mines persist in most of the world but especially in South Africa and Canada.

The asbestos fibers are valuable because they do not burn; they resist chemicals, water and electricity. Much like lead, the fibers last nearly forever. Because the fibers are so resistant, they had many industrial uses in gaskets, brake linings, fire protection for building interiors (the World Trade Centers were filled with asbestos), shipbuilding, textiles and so on. Since asbestos is a fiber, it can be woven separately (as a fire suit) or combined with other fibers. In sum, asbestos is everywhere in our lives, some visible and others not so visible.

The first asbestos fibers were discovered in the Stone Age. The fact that asbestos does not burn made it a product of choice for war materials throughout the Dark Ages in Europe. Marco Polo discovered asbestos that was mined in China.

Asbestos came into its own in the industrial revolution of the 1800s. By the early 1900s, mines around the world were delivering more than 30,000 tons per year. That had grown to 109,000 tons in 1910. To fast forward, asbestos demand remained strong particularly in World War I and later World II. Asbestos reached its peak in 1973 with 804,000 tons per year. Asbestos use continued apace until its hazards were fully appreciated. In 2002, the last active U.S. asbestos mine was closed.

The many diseases from exposure to asbestos were slow to be discovered, much less embraced with corrective action. There were reasons for this delay, although with 20/20 hindsight, much should have been done earlier. The signature disease, mesothelioma, requires a long latency period to become disabling and then deadly. In the early days, when life expectancy was not as long as it is today, many asbestos miners and asbestos workers were dying of other causes before the disease had fully developed. In addition, much of the mining was done in poor countries where mines were plentiful, labor was cheap and worker safety was considered unimportant. Further, the call to use asbestos in products was overpowering. Many industries were demanding it. Its use was everywhere. If a few workers got sick and died, it was just considered a cost of doing business. That said, by the 1970s the relationship between lung diseases and asbestos came into clear view. By the 1980s, asbestos demand was declining, and insurance premiums for asbestos related diseases were soaring. The age of raw asbestos use was closing.

The health risks of asbestos became recognized worldwide. In 2003, 17 countries enacted asbestos bans. The U.S. was not one of them. There have been fifteen asbestos limiting bills filed in Congress, but none have passed. The EPA issued a ban on asbestos in 1989, but a lawsuit challenging it was filed; the law was overturned by the Fifth Circuit Court of Appeals in New Orleans, Louisiana. Over all these years, the U.S. was a small producer of asbestos but the largest consumer. As a result, large numbers of workers, in a broad spectrum of industries, worked with asbestos. They were exposed to asbestos fibers. Potentially, millions may have been exposed and will suffer one or more of the diseases and cancers that now lay at asbestos's doorstep. How the U.S. will care for and compensate them is an overwhelming dilemma.

Enter the lawyers. There was much work to do because Congress had stuck its head in the sand. Lawsuits began in the 1970s and grew quickly. Dozens of companies, large and small, have been forced into bankruptcy. Insurance policies have been exhausted. Tens of billions of dollars have been paid to law firms on both sides. The claims and lawsuits are not close to concluding. There are more claims to bring, so there must be more companies to find and sue. In sum, the Asbestos Litigation in the U.S. is a bear. A huge, ill-tempered bear. It has been on-going for over 40 years. It may go on for another 40 years.

My work in asbestos was limited to two years beginning in 2007. After I retired, I was called back by the former General Counsel of ICI PLC, now working for a London conglomerate that owned the Crane Company in Chicago. Crane is an old gasket manufacturer. Gaskets have wide use in engines and piping because they prevent leaks between steel joints. The gasket is sealed between the flanges or joints to make a secure fit. Crane made asbestos gaskets for many years and its gaskets were used in the first moon module. Crane, along with the other gasket companies, used asbestos as the preferred product for making gaskets for years. It was strong, heat resistant and lasted a long time. It was perfect for gaskets used in ships plus its hazards were not yet known. But after years of using them, mesothelioma claims among the shipyard workers began occurring.

Crane had tens of thousands of asbestos claims pending against it by workers that may have used its gaskets and now had mesothelioma. I moved to Chicago to reorganize its defenses, review and change some of the law firms defending it across the country and recover more of its insurance. This work took two years.

Everyday there is at least one asbestos trial occurring somewhere in the U.S. Moreover, there exists asbestos litigation "hell holes" in various U.S. cities. In such places, lawsuits are rampant, and verdicts are high. In Baltimore, shipyard workers used asbestos to build ships — a lot of ships — for many years. Ships require a lot of gaskets. Baltimore has a large population of shipyard workers and the latency years of asbestos exposure are expiring. Mesothelioma among these shipyard workers was becoming prevalent. Law firms specializing in asbestos lawsuits were thriving there. There may be thousands of asbestos claims in Baltimore requiring lawsuits.

I participated in one asbestos trial with Tom Burns, one of Crane's lead defense lawyers. It was in Baltimore, Maryland where a large number of ships had been built with Crane gaskets. Baltimore had become a center for asbestos lawsuits with million-dollar verdicts occurring regularly. Crane had previously lost asbestos trials there for millions.

There are basically three defenses available to a gasket company in an asbestos trial. First, there are differences in asbestos fibers so you can try to prove the worker's exposure was from someone else's gasket fiber — the same defense in The Station Club. This requires microscopic examination of fiber remnants found in the lungs on autopsy. But pathologists often disagree on the findings. Second, you can discover purchasing records showing other gasket suppliers. But a number of gasket makers had gone out of business so blaming others was problematic. Third, you can discover the worker was employed by other employers that did not use Crane products and his exposure occurred there. But there is no defense to the claim that the worker's death was caused by asbestos exposure, *i.e.* mesothelioma.

An asbestos trial usually lasts less than two weeks. Many of the key witnesses (pathologists and records custodians) for both sides testify often; they are, in fact, well paid professional testifying asbestos experts. The Baltimore judge in our case had conducted other asbestos trials. The juries in Baltimore were used to finding the defendants, including Crane, liable and often assessing millions in damages. The community was sympathetic to the workers.

I learned first-hand the difficulties of winning an asbestos trial where the innocent working man has died, or worse, is dying in the courtroom from mesothelioma. In our case, the plaintiff had recently died a painful and tragic death. He had worked for the same shipbuilder for 34 years. Crane's defense was based on a tiny, microscopic fiber found on autopsy and the fact that a number of different companies sold the gaskets that the worker used. Those defenses failed in the jury's eyes. We lost our trial, but the verdict was not unexpected, a million dollars.

The history of addressing the asbestos problem in England is quite different from the U.S. In the U.S., the asbestos problem became recognized by litigation in the 1970s. It has grown exponentially since then. By comparison, England began addressing the problem seriously in the 1960s, ten years earlier. Rather than only litigation, the British government responded with social support and victim payment regimes. By 2012, according to "Asbestos Compensation in England," these regimes included: Disability Living Allowance, Constant Attendance Allowance, Exceptionally Severe Disablement Benefit, Statutory Sick Pay, Employment and Support Allowance and the Carer's Allowance. The comparison to the failure to respond in the U.S. is striking.

The asbestos litigation in England also has marked differences from the U.S. First, proving a claim was eased by a court decision in 1931 finding asbestos control was the employer's duty, *stare decisis*. This is the common law of the land. The employer is defenseless against his employee's claim. In the U.S., lawsuits by employees against their employers are not permitted because of workers compensation statutes. Every state has such statutes. The problem is that the employees can, instead, sue the companies like Crane that made the gaskets, rather than their employer.

In England, there is no sympathetic jury to decide. The case belongs in total to an experienced judge. So, the trial is short and direct, without the need to convince a jury of citizens which side should win. Moreover, the damages awarded will be much smaller because England has government support which has been paid to the victim.

As you can see, the asbestos litigation conundrum in the U.S. defies solution. Surely, there is a better way.

OTHER MASS TORT LAWSUITS

The Mass Torts I have described so far are some of the largest and most complex cases of the time. But the cases were only part of this large Mass Tort iceberg. Litigation was expanding into many areas. So, there were many other Mass Tort problems to be resolved. I defended some of them as well. I will review three, briefly.

FIRESTONE TIRES AND RIMS

Both Firestone 500 Tires and Firestone Multi-Piece Rims produced hundreds of lawsuits in the 1980s. The tire claims were alleged to be caused by manufacturing defects in popular radial tires, *i.e.* the rubber did not properly adhere to the metal belts within the tire. Under this alleged theory, when the rubber and belt separated, the tire came apart and failed — causing an accident. The tire was then alleged in a lawsuit to have been defectively made causing it to disintegrate and fail, often at high speeds. In fact, this was rarely true. Most of the tire accidents were caused by driver abuse of the tire and gross under inflation. At expressway speeds, an under inflated tire flexes excessively, overheats and then the rubber separates and fails, often causing high-speed accidents. There were numerous Firestone 500 tire lawsuits. The Firestone defense team and I won more cases than we lost at trial, and many were settled for defense costs. But a citizen jury is clearly not the best judge of tire manufacturing and thermal science.

Firestone manufactured multi-piece steel rims for large truck and school bus wheels for decades. Most of the claims occurred when a service station employee was working to inflate a tire with the high air pressure required for truck tires.

If the rims' two-piece flanges were not engaged and joined together tightly when preparing the rim for attaching and inflating the tire, they could separate as the air pressure rises and causes the tire to stress the wheel. The rims will then come apart if not properly locked together and the high air pressure explosion can be deadly or maiming. These severe accidental injuries were caused by the worker's failure to both properly engage the rim flanges during assembly and to safely use the available steel cages and/or chains to contain a forceful separation. These items were provided at service stations where the workers were changing truck tires but were often disregarded.

Firestone assembled a group of lawyers across the country to defend it in the hundreds of rim lawsuits. Because many of the rims were old and wearing out, explosions were occurring. I was retained to defend rim explosion lawsuits filed in Kentucky.

At the height of these claims, CBS's *60 Minutes* did a TV segment allegedly showing the dangers of the multi-piece truck rims. In the experiment they conducted in front of the CBS cameras, they used a plastic dummy who appeared to be working on the truck tire and inflating it. The rim forcefully separated, exploded and blew the dummy violently across the room. This made the dangers of the multi-piece rims seem obvious and conclusive. Plaintiff lawyers presented the *60 Minutes* video of this rim explosion as evidence of the rims' defective design in their jury trials. We obtained the video and looked at it frame by frame. We determined that something was wrong with the way this was being presented. We took discovery depositions under oath of the CBS employees who had prepared and conducted the experiment. They admitted that they could not get the rims to separate for the video presentation. The flanges always remained locked together. So, they used large steel files and filed down the flanges on the rims to the point where they could not fully engage with each other. Thus, the multi-piece rim they exhibited would blow apart explosively every time. The flanges could not be fully locked together. In essence, the *60 Minutes* program was a total misrepresentation of the truck rim performance. With this admission by CBS, the video was barred in future trials. Nevertheless, the fake segment had done a significant amount of harm in the litigation.

Because in almost every lawsuit, the workmen had failed to use the available cages and steel chains as a safety device, their negligence contributed to the cause of the accidents and injuries. In states that had contributory negligence as an absolute defense, this claim would be barred. In states that had comparative negligence, a failure to use the available devices would be set off against the claim that the multi-piece rim was itself defective. A percentage of fault by both the employee and Firestone could be assigned by the jury. As we developed our defenses, we discovered that most of the multi-piece rim cases involved old rims that had rusted over time. This rust impaired their ability to make a seal on each other. The rust was obvious, so those rims should have been discarded and not used. Using those rims was the fault of the worker.

I tried two of Firestone's cases in Kentucky. Since Kentucky at the time had contributory negligence as a defense, I won my first trial. In the second trial I succeeded with a cost of defense settlement before it was sent to the jury. Firestone's national defense attorney team won most of the trials. Over time, many older rims were discarded, and service station truck tire changers became educated to always use the chain and cage restraints. As a result, future cases were avoided.

GENERAL ELECTRIC APPLIANCES

In the 1990s, General Electric Company ("G.E.") produced a new refrigerator with an innovative rotary compressor. It was smaller and more efficient than the common, larger, piston driven compressors. The smaller compressor made more room in the refrigerator and used less electricity, a significant advantage. The new G.E. refrigerator sold well and was a success. But over time, mysterious fires began to occur around the refrigerators. Soon dozens of fire damage claims turned into lawsuits in seven states. In Beaumont, Texas, two elderly Texans died from a kitchen fire while sleeping upstairs at night. They were not wearing their hearing aids and were unaware of the smoke alarm. A G.E. refrigerator was in their kitchen.

Jack Welch, the CEO of G.E., acted decisively and undertook a massive recall. G.E. located each unit and changed out all of the rotary compressors in G.E. refrigerators across the entire U.S. The task was accomplished with remarkable speed. Soon there were no new claims, so the lawsuits ended. G.E. was so successful in showing good product stewardship that over the next two years their refrigerator sales increased by 32 percent. Harvard Business School embraced this decision and GE's behavior for a case study of excellence. In this situation, the "law of unintended consequences" produced a positive result.

Meanwhile, my team and I were directed to resolve the litigation already pending across the country. Our key to a successful defense was to avoid the consolidation of the lawsuits into a class action Mass Tort. We argued that the cause of every kitchen fire was contested so there was no commonality. Our argument succeeded. Each case stood on its own footing going forward.

We created a responsive settlement facility with G.E.'s insurer to address claims that were not yet lawsuits and we settled them. We then undertook to defend each and every lawsuit — there are other fire hazards in a kitchen we could point to. I started two G.E. trials, one in Bangor, Maine, and the other in Houston, Texas, but each settled before closing arguments. In the end, we settled all the cases. It was all covered by the G.E. insurance policy with Electric Mutual

Insurance Company with no adverse verdicts. No two lawsuits were ever consolidated.

The precise cause of the fires in the rotary compressor box was difficult to determine. Remember, fire destroys evidence. We believed it was a fault with the electrical switch device and wiring harness, manufactured by Murata Manufacturing Company, LTD, a huge Japanese trading company. We invited Murata to a meeting at G.E. Appliance Park in Louisville, Kentucky. Four Japanese executives arrived in a stretch limousine. We confronted them with our evidence and theories of fire causation by their product. We ultimately obtained a partial settlement from them. All the cases were finally resolved, and the matter was closed.

ORTHOPEDIC BONE SCREWS

In the 1990s, we also defended Youngwood Medical Specialties, Inc. of Pittsburg, Pennsylvania. They produced surgical screws for orthopedic applications. But lawsuits began around the country in cases where the screws, intended only for use in orthopedic surgery, were being used by neurosurgeons on steel spinal support structures made by Sofamor Danek. This was an "off label" use, where the doctor makes an individual, per case decision to do something in a different way than the product is designed for. This is permitted by the Food and Drug Administration. But sometimes after these surgeries the spinal structure would fail, and the result was devastating as the vertebrae collapsed. Youngwood did not sell the screws for this use; the neurosurgeon chose to do it "off label."

Youngwood was still sued in many cases across the country. The federal cases ended up consolidated in a proceeding in Philadelphia before judge Bechtel; state court lawsuits proceeded independently. In conjunction with Sofamor Danek we defended all the cases. I appeared in the other courts, often presenting motions in a number of states.

We tried one of the lawsuits in Philadelphia, an inner-city courtroom where juries were notorious for big verdicts against corporations. Although we lost the weeklong jury trial, on post-trial motions the Circuit Judge entered a judgment notwithstanding the verdict dismissing the case (the same result as in Yonkers). So, we paid the plaintiff nothing. After all, the screws were not intended for this use.

After three years, we concluded our defense of Youngwood by paying an insurance funded cost of defense settlement directly to Sofamor Danek. It indemnified Youngwood and assumed the defense of all the remaining cases filed against it.

This litigation was also illusory. Youngwood's manufacture of screws was never challenged as being defective. Rather, they were wrongfully accused of participating in the spinal structure surgery decision that had failed. That was not true. No neurosurgeon ever consulted Youngwood. Youngwood should have recovered all of its costs, attorney fees and the settlement — a sum in the millions — for the defense from the plaintiffs who sued it. That is only possible in England but not in the U.S.

These examples exhibit only a small part of what was occurring nationally and continues.

MASS TORTS TODAY

Today, Mass Tort litigation is alive, well and overwhelming. Two recent Mass Tort cases which I noted are of interest. In 2018, in St. Louis, Missouri, Johnson & Johnson defended a lawsuit by 22 women claiming its talcum powder caused their ovarian or cervical cancer. The defense included the FDA's approval of the product and many scientific articles supporting the safety of the product. Moreover, it has been used for nearly100 years by millions of women and babies without any known problems. Nevertheless, the jury awarded the plaintiffs $4.6 billion. As a result, many more women are now filing lawsuits.

In the same year, in San Francisco, California, a groundskeeper, who claimed the widely used weed killer Roundup caused his cancer, sued Monsanto. Monsanto's defense included 800 scientific articles supporting its safety, disproving the claim. Nevertheless, the jury returned a verdict of $286 million. Monsanto's defense of Roundup is expanding. A second verdict, for $87 million, occurred in Denver, Colorado. A Louisville, Kentucky newspaper, *The Courier-Journal*, reported that there are now more than 11,000 claims; an estimate for settlement of these cases was reported as approximately $5 billion.

Medical science is still debating whether there is "causation" of any cancer on the part of either talcum powder or Roundup. Ordinary juries hearing Mass Tort cases often lack the qualifications to understand the intricate and sophisticated medical science necessary to make accurate science-based decisions. They can, however, decide which expert witness and/or lawyer they like best. As large corporations, Johnson & Johnson and Monsanto face a bias against them in these jury trials. Are these two cases proceeding down the same path as the Silicone lawsuits, where wrongful litigation against a blameless product produced extreme costs and bankruptcies but rewarded lawyers?

A third huge Mass Tort is based on the opioid crisis. It seems reasonable to assume that with so many deaths, addictions and serious medical problems, there is a quantity of fault to be assigned to those in the manufacturing, distribution and prescription chain. Looking at this litigation is mindful of the tobacco litigation that was fought by the tobacco industry for decades. That defense largely collapsed when the states joined together to become plaintiffs. Thus, tens of billions of dollars in settlements were recovered for smokers and to create advertising of smoking hazards. Even so, today the lawsuits continue, advertisements about the dangers of smoking notwithstanding. This may also be the final opioid result years from now.

The news cycle reports daily on a new Mass Tort lawsuit, filed somewhere in the United States. Often more than one appears. Mass Tort cases are thriving. That said, finding accurate statistics in order to recite their massive volume is nearly impossible for a host of reasons. The reporting of total case numbers is specific to how the count is made. For example, some report on the large number of individual lawsuits combined into the Mass Tort definition, as in Philadelphia. Other reporters record the Mass Tort lawsuits as a single, combined "event," as a Lexis search reveals. This difference is dramatic! For instance, the MGM Grand was a Mass Tort. Once consolidated, Lexis would report it as one "Mass Tort case." But, in fact, there were 1,327 filed lawsuits arising from the "event" packed into the consolidated proceeding. Arguably, as in Philadelphia, you could report that there were 1,327 Mass Tort lawsuits.

Lexis is a recognized legal search engine. In 2018, Lexis reported 4,377 Mass Tort cases pending in 13 states (apparently 37 states do not even bother to keep this statistic). Pennsylvania is recited in the Lexis reporting group with 27 cases listed. At the same time, Philadelphia's Complex Litigation Center tracks Mass Tort lawsuit filings in Philadelphia only — just the one city in Pennsylvania. It reports 10,984 lawsuits in 2018. That is 10,957 more than Lexis reported. For my purposes, it is obvious that Mass Tort cases today, across the U.S., are not only vexatious but also too massive to even try to count.

Moreover, looking at the Philadelphia Complex Litigation Center, another statistic is troubling. It reports 4,280 Mass Tort/Complex Litigation lawsuits in 2010, and 10,984 in 2018. This is an increase of 256% over eight years. If that explosive trend continues, there will be 28,119 Mass Tort lawsuits pending in the city of Philadelphia alone in 2026. These growing numbers are consistent with the predictable growth of 320,000 more lawyers in the U.S. over the same eight-year time period. The expanding U.S. litigation conundrum is dire, indeed.

Another issue confusing the numbers counting is the definition of a "Mass Tort." It can also vary. The better term is "mass tort/complex litigation." This encompasses all class actions, not just those caused by Torts. Recent examples are the bank mortgage cases and the credit card "fraud" lawsuits; in each, the allegedly injured citizens were in the millions. While my experience focused only on Torts, adding together all complex litigations, as well, tells the true story.

When we look at all the Mass Torts claims that are reported, is there any question that litigation in the U.S. is beyond understanding and spiraling out of control? We are, indeed, a nation of lawyers.

The tragic events and products producing my cases, and others, demonstrate, to even a casual observer, that something is wrong with the U.S. legal system. No one looking for a "just, speedy and inexpensive" civil justice system (which the Federal Rules of Civil procedure require) would tolerate any one of them, much less all of them together. Part and parcel of this problem is the advent of lawyer advertising and the excessive number of lawyers in America.

ADVERTISING BY LAWYERS

Law students in America are required to take a legal ethics course in law school and pass the Multistate Professional Responsibility Examination before being admitted to the practice of law. It is a standardized exam on the ethics of lawyers and judges. Fidelity to our clients, diligence in advice, courtesy to our fellow lawyers, respect for the judges, a high standard of professional conduct and no solicitation of clients or advertising were all requisites when I started law practice.

In 1908, the American Bar Association Canons of Professional Ethics banned all advertising. In 1977, all of that was eroded. The U.S. Supreme Court, in the case of *Bates v. Arizona State Bar*, 433 U.S 350 (1977), ruled that the First Amendment permitted lawyers to advertise. Particularly, the Court rejected the argument that lawyer advertising is "inherently misleading" and "tarnish[es] the dignified public image of the profession."

Today, that Supreme Court decision is inexplicable, indeed. It was a 5-4 split decision with Mr. Justice Blackmun writing the majority Opinion, supporting a lawyer ad for a "routine divorce." His Opinion relies on an earlier decision allowing a pharmaceutical to be advertised for a stated price. But that connection makes little sense. A bottle of pills, like a sweater, candy bar or car is a "product" that can be sold to everyone for the same listed price, just ask Amazon. The advice of a lawyer is not a "product" but a professional opinion, as is the advice or diagnosis of a doctor. They are not sold on Amazon. Everyone cannot buy professional services for the same price.

Mr. Justice Blackmun's Opinion expressly approved a lawyer ad for a "routine divorce for $125.00." But divorce cases are complicated, never "routine." They involve complex issues of deciding child custody, support and visitation, identifying and dividing marital property, determining the payment of alimony, if at all, and much more. Each and every divorce is dependent upon discovering numerous facts and attitudes, then deciding how they impact the often-contentious parties and resulting legal issues. A stated fee for every individual to get a "routine divorce" is senseless. Apparently, none of the five Justices had ever purchased a divorce.

Moreover, Mr. Justice Blackmun anticipated he was opening the door wide to the potential for lawyer advertising abuses. So, in his Opinion he designated the 50 state bar associations to "police" lawyer advertising in order to protect the public. That decision put the fox in charge of the henhouse. State bar associations are notorious for not disciplining their lawyers. I discuss this problem later in the chapter, Lawyer Discipline.

In sum, the existing prohibition on lawyer advertising in 1977 was long standing, universal and working well. Lawyers were trained to be "professionals." They were expected to act with a high degree of ethics, including not soliciting clients. Not one person in the general public was demanding lawyer ads. No one was challenging the existing prohibition, except for the self-interested lawyers that filed the lawsuit and engaged the Supreme Court.

It is enlightening to read the Dissenting Opinions of the four Justices in that decision, including highly regarded Mr. Chief Justice Burger. Mr. Justice Powell wrote a lengthy Dissenting Opinion taking the five Justices to task. He correctly predicted the mess that has occurred over the past four decades because of lawyer advertising. I will provide but a few of his many insights:

> *Although the Court appears to note some reservations (mentioned below) it is clear that within undefined limits today's decision will effect profound changes in*

the practice of law, viewed for centuries as a learned profession.

******

The average lay person simply has no feeling for which services are included in the package divorce, and thus no capacity to judge the nature of the advertised product.... In the end, it will promote distrust of lawyers and disrespect for our own system of justice.

*****

The Court seriously understates the difficulties, and over-estimates the capabilities of the bar or indeed of any agency public or private to assure with a reasonable degree of effectiveness that price advertising can at the same time be both unrestrained and truthful.

Mr. Chief Justice Burger, noting the need to protect the general public from unscrupulous lawyers, chimed in:

I particularly agree with Mr. Justice Powell's statement that "today's decision will effect profound changes in the practice of law." Although the exact effect of those changes cannot now be known, I fear they will be injurious to those whom the ban on legal advertising was designed to protect, the members of the general public in need of legal services.

******

To impose the enormous new regulatory burdens called for by the Court's decision on the presently deficient machinery of the bar and courts is unrealistic;

it is almost predictable that it will create problems of unmanageable proportions.

We can see today that the four dissenting Justices accurately foresaw the "law of unintended consequences." The other five Justices were blind and did not. So, by one more vote of a single Justice, lawyer advertising was set loose on the unsuspecting public in 1977.

This decision opened the door and although some efforts were made to place constraints on the content of ads, lawyers — particularly plaintiff contingency fee lawyers — ran with it. But remember, the five members of the Supreme Court, who allowed advertising, *are also lawyers*. Lawyers are known for looking after their own.

There are at least three insidious results from lawyer advertising. First, is the decline of professionalism as lawyers look more and more like car salesmen on television. Second, is that advertising obscures the ability of lay people to judge the quality of the lawyer they intend to employ. Third, advertising has expanded the numbers of people seeking lawyers to file meritless lawsuits.

When I graduated from law school in 1964, advertising and the solicitation of clients was prohibited. The lawyer referral service, which was tightly managed by the bar association, and referrals among lawyers, were prevalent. Thus, persons seeking a lawyer had resources available to determine who would be a good fit for the legal services they required. By and large, lawyers knew and thought well of each other. There were fewer lawyers then. Therefore, if you were a lawyer of average or poor ability, everyone knew it and we would often steer new clients to a lawyer better suited to meet their needs. While this system was not perfect, it worked perfectly well. Everyone acted professionally and worked hard to be respected. To be otherwise would place you at a disadvantage among your lawyer peers so your referrals would decline.

We know this referral system worked well. First, it existed for centuries. Second, I recall the approval rating by the public for lawyers in the early 1970s was 89 percent, only three percentage points below doctors at the time. In 2009, it was 23 percent[70]. It was 18 percent four years later[71]. It is lower now. I cannot say that the low approval rating is due entirely to lawyer advertising, but it certainly plays a role. A drop that significant is nothing to sneeze at.

The advertising *coup de gras* to legal professionalism has carried with it other negative aspects. The mutual respect among lawyers has declined, which has likely influenced the negative public approval ratings. Moreover, with the rating decline, clients and prospective clients are far more suspicious and less trusting of their lawyers. This leads to a decline in attorney/client mutual loyalty, which is aided and abetted by the existence of contingency fee contracts. An American Bar Association poll was particularly telling: it reported that 74 percent of those surveyed agreed that "lawyers are more interested in winning than in seeing that justice is served"; 69 percent believed "lawyers are more interested in making money than in serving their clients"; 57 percent claimed that "lawyers are more concerned with their own self-promotion than their client's best interests"; and more than half (51 percent) agreed that "we would be better off with fewer

[70] Staci Zaretsky, Lawyers: The Most Despised Profession in America, Above the Law (July 15, 2013) available at https://abovethelaw.com/2013/07/lawyers-the-most-despised-profession-in-america/ (last visited March 23, 2019) (In 2009, 23 percent of Americans surveyed say that lawyers contributed "a lot" to society).

[71] *Id.* (In 2013, 18 percent of Americans surveyed say that lawyers contributed "a lot" to society).

lawyers."[72]

Today, lawyer advertisements are ubiquitous. Large advertising budgets exist for large plaintiff's law firms. Television, radio, newspapers, magazines, billboards, buses all carry lawyer advertising. Many invite you to join others in litigating claims in a variety of areas. The result is that average citizens cannot discern the abilities of one lawyer or law firm from another. Does a slick ad present a good lawyer, or a good advertiser? Some lawyers still believe they are a cut above automobile salesmen. But does the public think so? Apparently not... except for that 18 percent.

Today, we exist in a "buyer beware" marketplace for legal services. This "pig in a poke" aspect for lawyers today belies the professionalism that existed in the past. Recently, *CBS News Sunday Morning* aired a critical report on lawyer advertising, stating that it is now a one-billion-dollar business. Is this what the Supreme Court had in mind?

---

[72] David VandeWaa, Overcoming the Negative Stigma Associated with Attorneys, LaFleur Marketing (October 11, 2016), available at https://lafleur.marketing/blog/overcoming-the-negative-stigma-associated-with-attorneys/.

LAWYERS, LAWYERS AND MORE LAWYERS

ONE MILLION FOUR HUNDRED THOUSAND U.S. LAWYERS

Lawyers are an interesting breed. They come in all shapes, sizes and abilities. They are generally intelligent because they graduated from college with grades and activities high enough to be accepted into a law school. They have taken and scored well on the standardized Law School Admission Test. They have attended law school for three years and then graduated. After law school they take and pass a multi-day bar examination. When they pass, they are licensed to practice law. While this places lawyers collectively in the upper percentage of the population as a whole in terms of education, it cannot be too difficult. After all, about 40,000 lawyers enter American society each year[73].

Lawyers like to congregate. Drop by your local courthouse some day and count all the dark suits, white shirts and red or blue ties. The explanation for this is apparent in your community. It is a truism well-known among lawyers. If a town has no lawyers, the townspeople and merchants adapt. They get along fine. They can manage their disputes among themselves. Then a single lawyer comes to town. He becomes known as "the starving lawyer." Why? Because the townspeople and merchants, as before, will continue to get

---

[73]Jeff Jacoby, *US Legal Bubble Can't Pop Soon Enough*, BOSTON GLOBE (May 9, 2014), https://www.bostonglobe.com/opinion/2014/05/09/the-lawyer-bubble-pops-not-moment-too-soon/qAYzQ823qpfi4GQl2OiPZM/story.html.

along. Who needs a lawyer?

Then a second lawyer comes to town. The first lawyer's income doubles. Why? Because some of the townspeople and merchants begin to distrust each other. One or more of them could be using a lawyer so he better use one too. The scale is tipping. They start to use lawyers.

Then two more lawyers come to town. The first lawyer's income doubles again. Now many townspeople and merchants are using lawyers. And so, it goes... on and on. Lawyers believe you can never have too many lawyers. If there is mischief to find, a lawyer will find it.

If you drive through any American community, you will find an Estate section. It is usually on a hill or hills, with views of a river, lake, ocean, forest or mountain. It has large lawns and luxurious homes. Who lives there? The town banker, a few merchants, a car dealer, a surgeon or two and a lot of lawyers. I rest my case.

The 1,400,000 lawyers in the U.S. are not only everywhere you look but also ever-present where America's laws are being made.[74] Their best defense to a challenge to thwart their mischief is to dominate and control where laws are made. For example, 62 percent of the United States Senate and 43 percent of Congress are lawyers.[75]

In state legislatures, the number of lawyers has declined over the last forty years.[76] That said, there still are a lot of lawyers in state legislatures. It is safe to opine that as a group,

---

[74] https://www.theatlantic.com/business/archive/2013/06/the-absolute-worst-states-for-job-hunting-law-school-grads/276463/; https://blogs.wsj.com/law/2012/11/19/more-law-schools-cut-class-size/.

[75] https://fas.org/sgp/crs/misc/R44762.pdf.

[76] Sahil Chinoy & Jessia Ma, *How Every Member Got to Congress*, N.Y. TIMES (Jan. 26, 2019), https://www.nytimes.com/interactive/2019/01/26/opinion/sunday/paths-to-congress.html; http://www.ncsl.org/research/about-state-legislatures/who-we-elect.aspx

there are more lawyer legislators than any other profession. Their influence is still present and important to the practicing lawyers. Remember, lawyers look after each other.

Further, the judges in the thousands of courts in the United States are licensed to be lawyers.[77] What are the chances that a state court judge, serving a six-year term and standing for re-election, will decide a case adverse to lawyering when he may have to return to lawyering after leaving the court?

The chart below compares the U.S. to other countries that endorse the rule of law. Let us look at 2010:

PER CAPITA LAWYERS BY COUNTRY (2010)			
COUNTRY	LAWYERS	POPULATION	RATIO
USA	1.2M	323M	1:260
USA – WASHINGTON D.C	50K	672K	1:12
JAPAN	23K	127M	1:5500
FRANCE	46K	67M	1:1500
ENGLAND	118K	65M	1:500
CHINA	165K	1.4B	1:7000

Based on this chart from 2010, the U.S. had as many lawyers as England, France, Japan and China combined, with 840,000 lawyers left over.

LAW SCHOOLS

Where do all these 40,000 lawyers come from each year? Universities discovered about 40 years ago that their law

[77] *See generally* Matt Ford, "When Your Judge Isn't a Lawyer," *The Atlantic* (Feb. 5, 2017), https://www.theatlantic.com/politics/archive/2017/02/when-your-judge-isnt-a-lawyer/515568/.

schools were potential cash cows. There was relatively small overhead involved in increasing the size of the law school classes. There was tuition to be made.

Universities could collect twice as much tuition by doubling the law school enrollment. All at a low cost. The law library was already in place and all that was needed was to add a few adjunct law professors – low salary, temporary positions. Cash flow followed. This is not possible for medical or engineering schools. They both require capital investments in fixed assets, technologies and labs. Law school does not.

Next was readily available law school financing. Graduate student loans entered the picture. Any aspiring law student could now easily borrow in excess of $100,000. Many borrowed much more than that to receive a law degree.

Lastly, each law school sets its own admission standards, so law schools were able to adjust the gate to enter law school. College graduates with liberal arts degrees can choose between teaching or lawyering. Which seems more attractive and remunerative? They also believe the higher salaries in law firms would facilitate the repayment of their student loans.

Law schools began graduating hordes of lawyers-to-be. Eventually the law of supply and demand caught up with new lawyers.[78] It became hard to find jobs in the better law firms unless your law school class standing, a more important measure than grades, was in the upper ten percent of the class. Job opportunities declined in proportion to class standing.[79]

---

[78] Catherine Rampell, "The Lawyer Surplus, State by State," *N.Y. TIMES* (June 27, 2011, 11:00am), https://economix.blogs.nytimes.com/2011/06/27/the-lawyer-surplus-state-by-state/?mtrref=www.google.com; *See* Joshua Wright, *Data Spotlight: New Lawyers Glutting the Market (Updated)*, EMSI (June 22, 2011), https://www.economicmodeling.com/2011/06/22/new-lawyers-glutting-the-market-in-all-but-3-states/.

[79] *Id.*

As an example, in 2007, about 91% percent of graduates joined law firms.[80] By 2013, only 51 percent were employed by law firms.[81] These percentages are better today.[82]

Undeterred, students keep applying while law schools continue to graduate as many law students as possible. The cash cow needs to be fed. The good news is that law school applications are declining. But like the snake that ate the pig and slowly digested its meal, it will be some time – if ever – before equilibrium between new lawyers and law jobs will be attained. Nevertheless, new lawyers are entering the profession at the rate of 40,000 each year. We are, indeed, a nation of lawyers.

LAWYER DISCIPLINE

All lawyers are subject to the Model Rules of Professional Responsibility. Each state's highest court promulgates rules for law practice. The state's bar association helps to manage the lawyers and oversee their law practice. Unfortunately, rogue lawyers are difficult to discipline because of the vagueness involved with enforcing these rules.[83] There are procedures required — legal hoops to jump through — to cause a discipline. Such discipline always runs the risk of disbarment. This means a lawyer accused of violating the

---

80 *Id.*

81 *Id.*

82 Stacy Zaretsky, "Job Market For Law School Grads Is 'Best Since the Recession, 'Bolstered by Biglaw Hiring," *Above the Law* (August 2, 2018), available at https://abovethelaw.com/2018/08/job-market-for-law-school-grads-is-best-since-the-recession-bolstered-by-biglaw-hiring/ (last visited April 13, 2019).

83 See Leslie C. Levin, "The Emperor's Clothes and Other Tales About the Standards for Imposing Lawyer Discipline Sanctions," 48 Am. U.L. Rev. 1, 8 (1998).

Model Rules will likely employ every means to fight the charge to avoid discipline.

Data on lawyer disbarments is hard to find. A most comprehensive survey was conducted in 2016 by the ABA's Center for Professional Responsibility.[84] According to the survey, there were about 100,000 lawyer complaints[85] received by disciplinary agencies across the country.[86] Of these, about 60 percent (60,000) of the complaints were investigated[87] but only six percent (6,000) of those investigations led to formal charges by disciplinary agencies.[88] Even more striking is that by the end of the year, only about

---

[84] Due to various reasons, the following states were not included in the survey: Alaska, Arkansas, California, Connecticut, Delaware, District of Columbia, Florida, Indiana, Maine, Massachusetts, Missouri, parts of New York, North Dakota, and Utah. *2016 Survey on Lawyer Discipline Systems (S.O.L.D.)*, ABA CTR. FOR PROF. RESP. (Jan. 2018), https://www.americanbar.org/content/dam/aba/administrative/professional_responsibility/2016sold_results.pdf.

[85] *2016 Survey on Lawyer Discipline Systems (S.O.L.D.)*, ABA CTR. FOR PROF. RESP. (Jan. 2018), https://www.americanbar.org/content/dam/aba/administrative/professional_responsibility/2016sold_results.pdf.

[86] This total includes statistics from the California Bar's public database. *See* Elizabeth R. Parker, *Annual Discipline Report*, The State Bar of California 10 (Apr. 30, 2017), http://www.calbar.ca.gov/Portals/0/documents/reports/2016_AnnualDisciplineReport.pdf?ver=2017-05-19-134141-270.

[87] *See 2016 Survey on Lawyer Discipline Systems (S.O.L.D.)*, ABA CTR. FOR PROF. RESP. (Jan. 2018), https://www.americanbar.org/content/dam/aba/administrative/professional_responsibility/2016sold_results.pdf; Elizabeth R. Parker, *Annual Discipline Report*, The State Bar of California 10 (Apr. 30, 2017), http://www.calbar.ca.gov/Portals/0/documents/reports/2016_AnnualDisciplineReport.pdf?ver=2017-05-19-134141-270.

[88] *id.*

1.5 percent (1,500) of the lawyers who were investigated were disbarred. [89] Since there were more than 1,400,000 practicing lawyers, that means only a very few, 1,500, were stopped from practicing.

A rogue lawyer can do great harm and sadly, it can take years to discipline him. One of my classmates became a plaintiff's lawyer. Although successful, his lifestyle exceeded his income. As a result, he represented a widow whose husband was killed in a trucking accident. He successfully prosecuted her claim and recovered a large settlement. Rather than advising her of the settlement, he kept it secret. Over time, he stole the proceeds of the settlement. At the end of the day, years later, he was found out, disbarred and went to prison. But that did not return all the monies from the large settlement to the widow.

Even if a lawyer has received some form of discipline, there is no certainty that he will change his ways; the system fails to effectively deter rogue lawyers. Remember, lawyers look after their own.

---

[89] *Id.*

THE COST OF LITIGATION IN AMERICA

Studies have shown that the cost of litigation in America greatly exceeds, by many times, the Eurozone and its partners.[90] The cost travels through our economy, emerging as a higher cost of insurance and manufactured products, compared to our foreign competitors.[91] This impact occurs in many ways. For example, when the Monsanto verdict came out, Dow DuPont, BASF, Bayer and MSCI U.S. Chemicals experienced a 25 percent drop in share prices. This response by the stock market is significant; it reflects the fear of potential new litigation against chemical companies.

In 2011, the cost of litigation was estimated at $264.6 billion or $857 per person in the U.S.[92] If that was true in 2011, it is probably more than double that today, approximately ten years later, and still growing. The doubled numbers would be over $500 billion dollars and nearly $2,000 per person.[93] Think about that number! *You are paying a $2,000 a year surcharge to lawyers* and perhaps much more. The exponential cost of U.S. litigation has very real and negative impacts on healthcare in the United States. Hospitals and doctors are spending money and resources on medical

---

[90] *See* David L. McKnight & Paul J. Hinton, *International Comparisons of Litigation Costs*, U.S. CHAMBER INST. FOR LEGAL REFORM (June 2013), https://www.instituteforlegalreform.com/uploads/sites/1/ILR_NERA_Study_International_Liability_Costs-update.pdf.

[91] *id.*

[92] *2011 Update on U.S. Tort Cost Trends*, TOWERS WATSON, https://www.casact.org/library/studynotes/Towers-Watson-Tort-Cost-Trends.pdf.

[93] *See Id.*

litigation and its anticipated defense rather than improving the quality of healthcare.[94] Liability costs (both actual and avoidance) is 27 percent.[95] If accurate, curbing the litigation could increase our healthcare by as much as one trillion dollars a year.

It is estimated that litigation cost makes up more than two percent of the United States gross domestic product, much higher than most other countries. Consider France, where that number is less than one percent (0.56 percent). It has an instructive system restraining lawsuits. To file a liability (Tort) lawsuit in France, the claim is first investigated by a government lawyer. If, after a review of its facts, circumstances and the applicable Code laws, he recommends a suit be filed, it is then submitted to a three-lawyer panel. If they also recommend it, the lawsuit for injuries and damages can be filed. The impact of such a review system on lawsuits in the U.S. would be beyond dramatic. I suggest that more than 50 percent of today's litigation could be avoided by such a review system. France also has the English Rule. This is a second check and balance built into the system to avoid wrongful lawsuits. Thus, pre-lawsuit settlements are encouraged and cost effective in France. They bring real cost savings to both sides and the country. Not so for us, a nation of lawyers.

---

[94] *See* Michelle M. Mello, Amitabh Chandra, Atul A. Gawande, & David M. Studdert, *National Costs of the Medical Liability System*, NIH, https://www.ncbi.nlm.nih.gov/pmc/articles/PMC3048809/pdf/nihms269333.pdf (last visited Mar. 20, 2019).

[95] *id.*

TORT REFORM: CAN THE LITIGATION ABUSES BE CORRECTED?

As the litigation train began to run off the tracks, efforts came forward to curb the abuses. These efforts began about four decades ago. They were labeled "Tort Reform." Over the years, they have been argued over and written about at great length. Today, Tort Reform is a vast and disputed subject, beyond the confines of this book. Nevertheless, I will explore the tip of this iceberg for your general understanding of it.

Those supporting Tort Reform argue that U.S. litigation is too expensive, lawyers receive more money from Tort lawsuits than the injured parties, frivolous lawsuits and class actions are excessive and expensive, and run-away juries award ridiculous amounts of damages. Those opposing Tort Reform argue that the litigation system is not broken and serves everyone who has been injured, insurance companies and corporations must be held accountable, and it amounts to corporate welfare at the expense of those who have been severely injured. A large body politic of lawyers oppose Tort Reform.

Some ways to achieve Tort Reform have emerged. One is to place pre-determined limits, or a "cap," on the damages awarded by juries. For example, a cap could be that an award for pain and suffering cannot exceed $500,000. The concept has gained some traction in the area of punitive damages. "Punitive damages" are awarded by the jury in addition to all other damages as punishment for what is intentional or egregious conduct. Other Tort Reform limiting opportunities include shortening the statute of limitations (the time in which a lawsuit must be filed), establishing a condition which must be met before a lawsuit can be filed (to file a medical malpractice suit you must first have a doctor's opinion supporting the claim), and other procedural issues.

In essence, there are two avenues to accomplish Tort Reform. The first, and by far largest, is through the passage of legislation. This track is both complex and convoluted because laws are enacted state-by-state. Thus, each state must adopt its own version of Tort Reform, if any. The result is there can be 50 different versions without any uniformity.

Because lawyers oppose Tort Reform, the fact that they often dominate state legislatures makes passing such laws difficult. Moreover, when legislation *is* passed, it is often challenged with lawsuits. In recent years, the courts in Wisconsin, North Dakota, Oregon, and Missouri have declared the Tort Reform statutes passed in their legislatures to be unconstitutional. The appellate courts of those states protected the lawyers.

What does the future for Tort Reform look like? Obviously, a host of lawyers successfully oppose Tort Reform. Moreover, lawyers are powerful, indeed. In 1964, the plaintiff's lawyers in the U.S. formed the "American Trial Lawyers Association" ("ATLA"), recently renamed the "American Association for Justice." Many believe it is one of the richest and best organized lobbying groups on the planet. ATLA has been active in opposing Tort Reform in every state, and especially the U.S. Congress. The U.S. Senate remains silent because more than 60% of the members are lawyers. Lawyers look after their own.

However, over time, there has been Tort Reform progress with some medical malpractice litigation. According to a 2010 Gallup poll, doctors were rated "excellent" by 83% of Americans. It remains that high today. That rating is many times higher than the public rating for lawyers (18%). The doctors and the American Medical Association can be a formidable opponent for the lawyers in ATLA. As a result, the Expert Institute reports that 29 states now have some manner of medical malpractice Tort Reform. Of course, that leaves 21 states like Wisconsin, Oregon, North Dakota and Missouri without it. In those states, the lawyers are still in control.

The second avenue to seek Tort Reform is through lawsuits in the courts, but success on this pathway is difficult and limited because lawyers reside there. That said, however, there has been some progress in the U.S. Supreme Court. The Supreme Court has focused, at times, on creating a "punitive damages cap." For nearly 20 years, it has periodically reviewed the constitutional issues presented by placing a cap on punitive damages. It finds some support in the 8th Amendment (prohibition against excessive fines) and the 5th and 14th Amendments (due process). This is a difficult journey for Tort Reform. The Supreme Court decides only the case before it; it does not legislate laws. Thus, the case it decides may be limited in scope or present a narrow issue. Reviewing and analyzing its decisions in this area is beyond the scope of this book. Many others have already written, and are still writing, books on this subject. Nevertheless, the Court has placed some "caps" on punitive damage awards.

You now see what a complex and contentious issue Tort Reform continues to be today. The U.S. litigation swamp is not likely to be drained by Tort Reform anytime soon.

THE U.S. SUPREME COURT: CASES AND THE FEDERAL RULES OF CIVIL PROCEDURE

As you have seen in previous chapters, lawyers challenged the common law for their benefit. Three of the aberrations (American Rule, Contingency Fees and Advertising) were created by lawsuits. They began in the trial court, then went to the appellate court and ultimately to the Supreme Court. There, the lawyers briefed and argued the issue before the nine Justices. The Supreme Court then issued its decision, and it was often a five to four vote. In those cases, one Justice's deciding vote let loose the problem on the unsuspecting public. The Supreme Court's decision in each case became the law of the land. So, the three decisions have been imbedded in U.S. common law, *stare decisis*, for a long time. Every federal court must follow them. The Supreme Court also governed the expansion of Class Actions in their Rule 38. Can the Supreme Court now reverse each decision and Rule 38 to change the law back to what it was before? The answer is a resounding, *yes*!

The Supreme Court is well known for overruling its own prior decisions. It has done so 233 times according to the *Government Publishing Office: Authenticated U.S. Government Information*. Think about that number, 233 times it decided its decision was wrong. So, it admits it makes mistakes regularly. This practice is further amplified in the report from the *Congressional Research Services: "The Supreme Courts Overruling of Constitutional Precedent"*, updated September 24, 2018 ("Report"). This Report of 26 pages cites recognized reasons utilized by the Supreme Court for overruling its wrong decisions. These reasons include "Workability" (*i.e.*, their past decision *is no longer working today*) and "Changed Understanding of Relevant Facts" (*i.e.*, the facts that served as the *basis for their past decision have changed* and are, hence, *no longer "relevant" today*). (Emphasis added.) As I have proven, litigation is out of control. It is not "working" for the good of the citizens and the "relevant facts" supporting it have changed, *dramatically*.

The Supreme Court's decisions in *Fleishman Distilling Corp*. enabling the American Rule, and *Bates* accepting Lawyer Advertising are not acceptable today. The facts have changed, and they do not work. We must assume the Supreme Court did not expect these results. The dissenting opinions predicted the mistakes the majority was making; these four Justices saw the future correctly.

Besides deciding new cases correcting its prior errors, the Supreme Court controls a second pathway to accomplish the same result. *No one can challenge its decisions.*

The Supreme Court promulgates the Federal Rules of Civil Procedure (this is their prerogative ceded to it by Congress in 28 U.S.C. Section 2071-2077 (1988)). It is the ultimate authority in all proceedings in the U.S. Court system:

> 28 U.S. Code Section 2072. Rules of procedure and evidence*; power to prescribe; (a) the Supreme Court shall have the power to prescribe general rules of practice and procedure* and rules of evidence for cases in the United States district court (including proceedings before magistrate judges thereof) and the courts of appeals. (Emphasis added.)

The Supreme Court's Rules already provide:

> "The Federal Rules of Civil Procedure govern civil proceedings in the United States district courts. *Their purpose is to secure the just, speedy, and inexpensive determination of every action and proceeding.*" Fed. R. Civ. P. 1. (Emphasis added).

This Rule was first adopted by order of the Supreme Court on December 20, 1937, transmitted to Congress on January 3, 1938, and effective September 16, 1938. Although periodically other Rules have been modernized and amended, Rule 1 still governs today.

The solution lies in the Supreme Court acknowledging that I am correct. Today, lawsuits are *unjust, slow and expensive*, the exact opposite of the Rule. They can undertake the corrective actions necessary to reform them. Once corrected, the states will largely follow, as thirty-five of the states have "adopted" the Federal Rules.

Amending the Federal Rules is the sole prerogative of the Supreme Court. It is a yearly process. It usually begins in the Judicial Conference of the United States. Thus, the Supreme Court can direct the Judicial Conference to address these issues. According to the official publication of the United States Courts:

> **Judicial Conference**
> *The Judicial Conference of the United States is the national policy making body for the federal courts.* (Emphasis added.) The current name took affect when Congress enacted Section 331 of Title 28 of the United States Code. Before that the body was known as the Conference of Senior Circuit Judges from its creation in 1922.
>
> **Circuit Judicial Councils**
> The council has *broad authority* with a statutory authorization to issue orders to promote accountability and "*the effective and expeditious administration of justice within its circuit.*" (Emphasis added.)

The Judicial Conference is the perfect place to start because it is comprised of Senior Circuit Judges. The U.S. Circuit Courts are the appellate courts that preside over the U.S.

District Courts (the jury trial courts), where the aberrations and abuses are occurring daily. The Senior Circuit Judges are not blind to what they are overseeing in the trial courts below them. *They have the power to redress the mess.*

CLOSING ARGUMENT

After the lawyers rest their respective cases in jury trials, it is time for their closing arguments. They sum up their evidence and argue the merits of their cases to persuade the jurors. Their goal is a favorable decision. In my experience, usually they ramble and argue too long. The closing statement should be like the old lady's dance, short and sweet. So, this will be short and to the point.

The power of the Supreme Court to either accept new cases to reverse its errors or enact new rules to correct its mistakes, is plenary (which means it cannot be challenged). If it decides to do so, it is game over for the lawyers' abuses.

So, by action rather than inaction, the tar pit can be cleaned. The decisions in *Fleishman* and *Bates* should be reversed. Class actions can be corrected by amending Federal Rule of Civil Procedure 38. The use of contingency fees can be returned to unethical and illegal conduct. Some limiting of the use of juries in all civil cases and restraining excessive damage awards can be reviewed, determined and supported under the U.S. Constitution. Lastly, the role of politics in selecting judges does not fall under the purview of the Supreme Court. Rather, the public must recognize and demand that politicians stop feathering their own nests but serve the public good. After all, isn't that why they were elected? Much of the English system can be adopted to select the best judicial candidates and not bicker over them.

Only one question remains: *Will the U.S. Supreme Court do what is right? Or will it continue to aid and abet a nation of lawyers?*

I now rest my case.

ACKNOWLEDGEMENTS

Lawyers are often called "word merchants." It is true. More words equal more time spent which equals larger hourly fees. Ever wonder why contracts and legal briefs are so long? Money. I have written my share of words in motions and briefs — but writing a book is a different genre — and much more difficult. I could not have written *Nation of Lawyers* without the endorsement and support of Barbara, my wife. She was my inspiration, collaborator and keen editor. She typed every word. Thank you, thank you.

I express recognition to LaQuasha Combs and Sue Eng Ly. They were senior law students at the Louis D. Brandeis School of Law at the University of Louisville, my alma mater. Their research and editing enhanced the end product. They will become excellent lawyers and I wish them every success.

In the 30 plus years that I defended Mass Tort litigations across the U.S., I was blessed to practice my cases with many co-defense lawyers, and against plaintiff's lawyers, who were the best lawyers in the country. I learned lessons from all of them. But not one of them was superior to the lawyers who worked with me from my Louisville law firm Brown, Todd & Heyburn. My special recognition and appreciation go to Winston Miller, Vic Maddox, Sue Wettle, Scott Dickens, Steve Embry, Hollis Wright, Lea Player, Steve Crawford, Rebecca Dernberger Wood, Colin Lindsey, Greg Belzley, Katie Yunker, John McCall, John Crockett, Dave Redmon, Bruce Baird, Mike Mercer, Sheryl Snyder, Lambert Farmer, Mary Ross Terry, Mark Feather and Doug Langdon. Each of you always gave me more than I asked of you. Special thanks also to Ed Glasscock, Managing Partner of the law firm. I always had whatever resources I needed to present the best defenses for our clients. Two who took care of me day after day and never sent me to the wrong city were Elaine Lamlein and Jane Cleary. Their devotion was special. Best of all was Cheri Dilliard *nee* Baird, my legal assistant without peer. She held everything together for me time after time. There is an expression, "When the going gets tough, the tough get going." She was tough, always going and gave me better than I deserved. To all, I say "Thank you!" More than you know. I could not have done it without you, and you made it a wonderful life experience in a wonderful time.

I also recognize both retired Judge William Stewart, and my former partner Vic Maddox, for their insights, perspective, critiques and recommendations which appear throughout the book.

Last, but not least, I am indebted to Tom Holbrook of RiverRun Bookstore. His advice, support, editing, and publishing made my story and book possible. Tom, I could not have done it without you. Thank you.

www.ingramcontent.com/pod-product-compliance
Lightning Source LLC
LaVergne TN
LVHW091640100826
845152LV00006B/110/J

* 9 7 8 1 9 5 0 3 8 1 8 2 1 *